Agent, Action, and Reason

This volume contains the papers and commentaries presented at the fourth philosophy colloquium held at the University of Western Ontario in November 1968. The papers examine, from different points of view, the central problems in the philosophy of action. They include: "Agency" by Donald Davidson with comments by James Cornman; "On the Logic of Intentional Action" by Roderick Chisholm with comments by Bruce Aune and a reply by Roderick Chisholm; "Wanting: Some Pitfalls" by R.M. Hare with comments by David Gauthier and D.F. Pears; "Two Problems about Reasons for Actions" by D.F. Pears with comments by Irving Thalberg. Also included is an extensive bibliography of recent work in the philosophy of action. The contributors are all well known for their work in this branch of philosophy; their papers present a cross section of the best work being done in the area at the present time.

ROBERT W. BINKLEY (PH D, University of Minnesota) is professor and assistant chairman of the department of philosophy at the University of Western Ontario. He studied under a Fulbright scholarship at Oxford University in 1956-7, and taught at Duke University for several years. His current research includes work on the use of model and tense logic in theory of action and in ethical theory. He is associate secretary of the Canadian Philosophical Association.

R.N. BRONAUGH (PH D, University of Wisconsin), associate professor of philosophy, has taught at the University of Western Ontario since 1962. He has published works in the area of responsibility and freedom.

AUSONIO MARRAS (PH D, Duke University) is assistant professor of philosophy at the University of Western Ontario. His main interests are the philosophy of mind, intentionality, and the history of philosophy.

Agent, Action, and Reason

EDITED BY

ROBERT BINKLEY, RICHARD BRONAUGH, AUSONIO MARRAS

UNIVERSITY OF TORONTO PRESS

© University of Toronto Press 1971
Reprinted in paperback 2014
ISBN 978-0-8020-1732-1 (cloth)
ISBN 978-1-4426-5190-6 (paper)
Microfiche ISBN 0-8020-0023-1
LC 71-151360

Acknowledgments

This volume contains the papers and comments presented at the Fourth University of Western Ontario Philosophy Colloquium, November 1-3, 1968, together with three additional items. These include two additional contributions by participants, for which the editors are very grateful: a reply to his commentator by Roderick Chisholm and a note on Hare's paper by D. F. Pears.

The final item is an extensive bibliography of recent work in the philosophy of action. A draft of the bibliography was distributed at the colloquium, and the editors wish to express their thanks to the many who made suggestions for its improvement.

Thanks also are due to the Canada Council for support in the preparation of the bibliography, to the British Council for assistance in bringing D. F. Pears to the colloquium, to S. G. French and C. D. Rollins for assistance in the original planning, and to the President, Dr. D. C. Williams, and other officers of the University of Western Ontario for making the colloquium possible at all.

Contents

Agent, Action, and Reason

1 / Agency*

Donald Davidson

What events in the life of a person reveal agency; what are his deeds and his doings in contrast to mere happenings in his history; what is the mark that distinguishes his actions?

This morning I was awakened by the sound of someone practising the violin. I dozed a bit, then got up, washed, shaved, dressed, and went downstairs, turning off a light in the hall as I passed. I poured myself some coffee, stumbled on the edge of the dining room rug, and spilled a bit of coffee fumbling for the *New York Times*.

Some of these items record things I did; others, things that befell me, things that happened to me on the way to the dining room. Among the things I did were get up, wash, shave, go downstairs, and spill a bit of coffee. Among the things that happened to me were being awakened and stumbling on the edge of the rug. A borderline case, perhaps, is dozing. Doubts could be kindled about other cases by

* Some of the ideas in this essay were formulated and tested in discussion with Irving Thalberg, to whom I am much beholden. Others who contributed to my thinking are Daniel Bennett, Joel Feinberg, Georg Kreisel, David Pears, and John Wallace. Thomas Nagel and George Pitcher generously and very helpfully commented on the penultimate draft. I am particularly indebted to James Cornman, some of whose comments at the symposium at which this paper was first read I have taken into account.

My research was aided by the National Science Foundation and the Center for Advanced Study in the Behavioral Sciences.

embroidering on the story. Stumbling can be deliberate, and when so counts as a thing done. I might have turned off the light by inadvertently brushing against the switch; would it then have been my deed, or even something that I did?

Many examples can be settled out of hand, and this encourages the hope that there is an interesting principle at work, a principle which, if made explicit, might help explain why the difficult cases are difficult. On the other side a host of cases raise difficulties. The question itself seems to go out of focus when we start putting pressure on such phrases as "what he did," "his actions," "what happened to him," and it often matters to the appropriateness of the answer what form we give the question. (Waking up is something I did, perhaps, but not an action.) We should maintain a lively sense of the possibility that the question with which we began is, as Austin suggested, a misguided one.[1]

In this essay, however, I once more try the positive assumption, that the question is a good one, that there is a fairly definite subclass of events which are actions. The costs are the usual ones: oversimplification, the setting aside of large classes of exceptions, the neglect of distinctions hinted by grammar and common sense, recourse to disguised linguistic legislation. With luck we learn something from such methods. There may, after all, be important and general truths in this area, and if there are how else will we discover them?

Philosophers often seem to think that there must be some simple grammatical litmus of agency, but none has been discovered. I drugged the sentry, I contracted malaria, I danced, I swooned, Jones was kicked by me, Smith was outlived by me: this is a series of examples designed to show that a person named as subject in sentences in the active, whether or not the verb is transitive, or as object in the passive, may or may not be the agent of the event recorded.[2]

---

1 See J. L. Austin, "A Plea for Excuses," in *Philosophical Papers* (Oxford: The Clarendon Press, 1961), pp. 126–127.
2 The point is developed in Irving Thalberg's "Verbs, Deeds and What Happens to Us," *Theoria*, 33 (1967), 259–260.

Another common error is to think verbs may be listed according to whether they do or do not impute agency to a subject or object. What invites the error is that this is true of some verbs. To say of a person that he blundered, insulted his uncle, or sank the *Bismark* is automatically to convict him of being the author of those events; and to mention someone in the subject position in a sentence with the verb in the passive tense is, so far as I can see, to ensure that he is not the agent. But for a host of cases, a sentence can record an episode in the life of the agent and leave us in the dark as to whether it was an action. Here are some examples: he blinked, rolled out of bed, turned on the light, coughed, squinted, sweated, spilled the coffee, and tripped over the rug. We know whether these events are actions only after we know more than the verb provides. By considering the additional information that would settle the matter, we may find an answer to the question of what makes a bit of biography an action.

One hint was given in my opening fragmentary diary. Tripping over a rug is normally not an action; but it is if done intentionally. Perhaps, then, being intentional is the relevant distinguishing mark. If it were, it would help explain why some verbs imply agency, for some verbs describe actions that cannot be anything but intentional; asserting, cheating, taking a square root, and lying are examples.

This mark will not work, however, for although intention implies agency, the converse does not hold. Thus spilling the coffee, sinking the *Bismark,* and insulting someone are all things that may or may not be done intentionally, but even when not intentional, they are normally actions. If, for example, I intentionally spill the contents of my cup, mistakenly thinking it is tea when it is coffee, then spilling the coffee is something I do, it is an action of mine, though I do not do it intentionally. On the other hand, if I spill the coffee because you jiggle my hand, I cannot be called the agent. Yet while I may hasten to add my excuse, it is not incorrect, even in this case, to say I spilled the coffee. Thus we must distinguish three situations in which it is correct to say I spilled the coffee: in the first, I do it intentionally; in the second I do not do it intentionally but it is my action (I thought it was tea); in the third it is not my action at all (you jiggle my hand).[3]

Certain kinds of mistake are particularly interesting: misreading a sign, misinterpreting an order, underestimating a weight, or miscalculating a sum. These are things that strictly speaking cannot be done intentionally. One can pretend to misread a sign, one can underestimate a weight through sloth or inattention, or deliberately write down what one knows to be a wrong answer to an addition; but none of these is an intentional flubbing. To make a mistake of one of the mentioned kinds is to fail to do what one intends, and one cannot, Freudian paradox aside, intend to fail. These mistakes are not intentional, then; nevertheless, they are actions. To see this we need only notice that making a mistake must in each case be doing something else intentionally. A misreading must be a reading, albeit one that falls short of what was wanted; misinterpreting an order is a case of interpreting it (and with the intention of getting it right); underestimating is estimating; and a miscalculation is a calculation (though one that founders).

Can we now say what element is common to the cases of agency? We know that intentional acts are included, and that the place to look to find what such acts share with the others is at the coffee spillings and such where we can distinguish spillings that involve agency from those that do not. I am the agent if I spill the coffee meaning to spill the tea, but not if you jiggle my hand. What is the difference? The difference seems to lie in the fact that in one case, but not in the other, I am intentionally doing *something*. My spilling the contents

3 This threefold division should not be confused with Austin's subtle work on the differences among purpose, intention, and deliberation in "Three Ways of Spilling Ink," *Philosophical Review*, 75 (1966), 427–440.

of my cup was intentional; as it happens, this very same act can be redescribed as my spilling the coffee. Of course, thus redescribed the action is no longer intentional; but this fact is apparently irrelevant to the question of agency.

And so I think we have one correct answer to our problem: a man is the agent of an act if what he does can be described under an aspect that makes it intentional.

The possibility of this answer turns on the semantic opacity, or intensionality, of attributions of intention. Hamlet intentionally kills the man behind the arras, but he does not intentionally kill Polonius. Yet Polonius is the man behind the arras, and so Hamlet's killing of the man behind the arras is identical with his killing of Polonius. It is a mistake to suppose there is a class of intentional actions: if we took this tack, we should be compelled to say that one and the same action was both intentional and not intentional. As a first step toward straightening things out, we may try talking not of actions but of sentences and descriptions of actions instead. In the case of agency, my proposal might then be put: a person is the agent of an event if and only if there is a description of what he did that makes true a sentence that says he did it intentionally. This formulation, with its quantification over linguistic entities, cannot be considered entirely satisfactory. But to do better would require a semantic analysis of sentences about propositional attitudes.[4]

Setting aside the need for further refinement, the proposed criterion of actions seems to fit the examples we have discussed. Suppose an officer aims a torpedo at a ship he thinks is the *Tirpitz* and actually sinks the *Bismark*. Then sinking the *Bismark* is his action, for that action is identical with his attempt to sink the ship he took to be the *Tirpitz*, which is intentional. Similarly, spilling the coffee is the act of a person who does it by intentionally spilling the contents of his cup. It is now clearer, too, why mistakes are actions, for making a

4 For an attempt at such a theory, see my "On Saying That," *Synthèse*, 19 (1968–69), 130–146.

mistake must be doing something with the intention of achieving a result that is not forthcoming.

If we can say, as I am urging, that a person does, as agent, whatever he does intentionally under some description, then, although the criterion of agency is, in the semantic sense, *intensional*, the expression of agency is itself purely *extensional*. The relation that holds between a person and an event when the event is an action performed by the person holds regardless of how the terms are described; and we can without confusion speak of the class of events that are actions, which we cannot do with intentional actions.

Perhaps it is sometimes thought that the concept of an action is hopelessly indistinct because we cannot decide whether knocking over a policeman, say, or falling down stairs, or deflating someone's ego is or is not an action. But if being an action is a trait which particular events have independently of how they are described, there is no reason to expect in general to be able to tell, merely by knowing some trait of an event (that it is a case of knocking over a policeman, say), whether or not it is an action.

Is our criterion so broad that it will include under actions many events that no one would normally count as actions? For example, isn't tripping over the edge of the rug just part of my intentional progress into the dining room? I think not. An intentional movement of mine did cause me to trip, and so I did trip myself: this was an action, though not an intentional one. But "I tripped" and "I tripped myself" do not report the same event. The first sentence is entailed by the second, because to trip myself is to do something that results in my tripping; but of course doing something that results in my tripping is not identical with what it causes.

The extensionality of the expression of agency suggests that the concept of agency is simpler or more basic than that of intention, but unfortunately the route we have travelled does not show how to exploit the hint, for all we have seen is how to pick out cases of agency by appeal to the notion of intention. This is to analyze the obscure by appeal to the more obscure – not as pointless a process as often thought, but still disappointing. We should try to see if we can find a mark of agency that does not use the concept of intention.

The notion of cause may provide the clue. With respect to causation, there is a certain rough symmetry between intention and agency. If I say that Smith set the house on fire in order to collect the insurance, I explain his action, in part, by giving one of its causes, namely Smith's desire to collect the insurance. If I say that Smith burned down the house by setting fire to the bedding, then I explain the conflagration by giving a cause, namely Smith's action. In both cases, causal explanation takes the form of fuller description of an action, either in terms of a cause or of an effect. To describe an action as one that had a certain purpose or intended outcome is to describe it as an effect; to describe it as an action that had a certain outcome is to describe it as a cause. Attributions of intention are typically excuses and justifications; attributions of agency are typically accusations or assignments of responsibility. Of course the two kinds of attribution do not rule one another out, since to give the intention with which an act was done is also, and necessarily, to attribute agency. If Brutus murdered Caesar with the intention of removing a tyrant, then a cause of his action was a desire to remove a tyrant and an effect was the death of Caesar. If the officer sank the *Bismark* with the intention of sinking the *Tirpitz*, then an action of his was caused by his desire to sink the *Tirpitz* and had the consequence that the *Bismark* sank.[5]

These examples and others suggest that, in every instance of action, the agent made happen or brought about or produced or authored the event of which he was the agent, and these phrases in turn seem rendered by the idea of cause.

5 In "Actions, Reasons, and Causes," *Journal of Philosophy*, 60 (1963), 685–700, I developed the theme that to give a reason or intention with which an action is performed is, among other things, to describe the action in terms of a cause. In this essay I explore how the effects of actions enter into our descriptions of them.

Can we then say that to be the author or agent of an event is to cause it? This view, or something apparently much like it, has been proposed or assumed by a number of recent authors.[6] So we should consider whether the introduction of the notion of causation in this way can improve our understanding of the concept of agency.

Clearly it can, at least up to a point. For an important way of justifying an attribution of agency is by showing that some event was caused by something the agent did. If I poison someone's morning grapefruit with the intention of killing him, and I succeed, then I caused his death by putting poison in his food, and that is why I am the agent in his murder. When I manage to hurt someone's feelings by denigrating his necktie, I cause the hurt, but it is another event, my saying something mean, that is the cause of the hurt.

The notion of cause appealed to here is ordinary event-causality, the relation, whatever it is, that holds between two events when one is cause of the other. For although we say the agent caused the death of the victim, that is, that he killed him, this is an elliptical way of saying that some act of the agent – something he did, such as put poison in the grapefruit – caused the death of the victim.

Not every event we attribute to an agent can be explained as caused by another event of which he is agent: some acts must be primitive in the sense that they cannot be analyzed in terms of their causal relations to acts of the same agent. But then event-causality cannot in this way be used to explain

6 For example, Roderick Chisholm, "Freedom and Action," in *Freedom and Determinism*, edited by Keith Lehrer (New York: Random House, 1966); Daniel Bennett, "Action, Reason and Purpose," *The Journal of Philosophy*, 62 (1965), 85–96; Anthony Kenny, *Action, Emotion and Will* (London: Routledge & Kegan Paul, 1963); Georg Henrick von Wright, *Norm and Action* (London: Routledge & Kegan Paul, 1963); Richard Taylor, *Action and Purpose* (Englewood Cliffs, NJ:Prentice-Hall, 1966). Previous criticism of this kind of causal analysis of agency can be found in my "The Logical Form of Action Sentences," in *The Logic of Decision and Action*, edited by Nicholas Rescher (Pittsburgh: University of Pittsburgh Press, 1967) and Irving Thalberg, "Do We Cause our Own Actions?" *Analysis*, 27 (1967), 196–201.

the relation between an agent and a primitive action. Event-causality can spread responsibility for an action to the consequences of the action, but it cannot help explicate the first attribution of agency on which the rest depend.[7]

If we interpret the idea of a bodily movement generously, a case can be made for saying that all primitive actions are bodily movements. The generosity must be open-handed enough to encompass such "movements" as standing fast, and mental acts like deciding and computing. I do not plan to discuss these difficult examples now; if I am wrong about the precise scope of primitive actions, it will not affect my main argument. It is important, however, to show that in such ordinary actions as pointing one's finger or tying one's shoelaces the primitive action is a bodily movement.

I can imagine at least two objections to this claim. First, it may be said that, in order to point my finger, I do something that causes the finger to move, namely contract certain muscles; and perhaps this requires that I make certain events take place in my brain. But these events do not sound like ordinary bodily movements. I think that the premisses of this argument may be true, but that the conclusion does not follow. It may be true that I cause my finger to move by contracting certain muscles, and possibly I cause the muscles to contract by making an event occur in my brain. But this does not show that pointing my finger is not a primitive action, for it does not show that I must do something else that causes it. Doing something that causes my finger to move does not cause me to move my finger; it *is* moving my finger.

In discussing examples like this one, Chisholm has sug-

---

7 Here, and in what follows, I assume that we have set aside an analysis of agency that begins by analyzing the concept of intention, or of acting with an intention, or of a reason in acting. These concepts can be analyzed, at least in part, in terms of event-causality. In the article mentioned in footnote 5, I try to show that although beliefs and desires (and similar mental states) are not events, we can properly say that they are causes of intentional actions, and when we say this we draw upon the concept of ordinary event-causality ("Actions, Reasons, and Causes," pages 693–695).

gested that, although an agent may be said to make certain cerebral events happen when it is these events that cause his finger to move, making the cerebral events happen cannot be called something that he does. Chisholm also thinks that many things an agent causes to happen, in the sense that they are events caused by things he does, are not events of which he is the agent. Thus if moving his finger is something a man does, and this movement causes some molecules of air to move, then although the man may be said to have caused the molecules to move, and hence to have moved the molecules, this is not something he did. [8]

It does not seem to me that this is a clear or useful distinction: all of Chisholm's cases of making something happen are, so far as my intuition goes, cases of agency, situations in which we may, and do, allow that the person did something. When a person makes an event occur in his brain, he does not normally know that he is doing this, and Chisholm seems to suggest that for this reason we cannot say it is something that he does. But a man may even be doing something intentionally and not know that he is; so of course he can be doing it without knowing that he is. (A man may be making ten carbon copies as he writes, and this may be intentional; yet he may not know that he is; all he knows is that he is trying.)

Action does require that what the agent does is intentional under some description, and this in turn requires, I think, that what the agent does is known to him under some description. But this condition is met by our examples. A man who raises his arm both intends to do with his body whatever is needed to make his arm go up and knows that he is doing so. And of course the cerebral events and movements of the muscles are just what is needed. So, though the agent may not know the names or locations of the relevant muscles, nor even know he has a brain, what he makes happen in his brain and muscles when he moves his arm is, under one natural description, something he intends and knows about.

8 Chisholm, "Freedom and Action."

The second objection to the claim that primitive actions are bodily movements comes from the opposite direction: it is that some primitive actions involve more than a movement of the body. When I tie my shoelaces, there is on the one hand the movement of my fingers, and on the other the movement of the laces. But is it possible to separate these events by calling the first alone my action? What makes the separation a problem is that I do not seem able to describe or think how I move my fingers, apart from moving the laces. I do not move my fingers in the attempt to cause my shoes to be tied, nor am I capable of moving my fingers in the appropriate way when no laces are present (this is a trick I might learn). Similarly, it might be argued that when they utter words most people do not know what muscles to move or how to hold their mouths in order to produce the words they want; so here again it seems that a primitive action must include more than a bodily movement, namely a motion of the air.

The objection founders for the same reason as the last one. Everything depends on whether or not there is an appropriate description of the action. It is correctly assumed that unless the agent himself is aware of what he is doing with his body alone, unless he can conceive his movements as an event physically separate from whatever else takes place, his bodily movements cannot be his action. But it is wrongly supposed that such awareness and conception are impossible in the case of speaking or of tying one's shoelaces. For an agent always knows how he moves his body when, in acting intentionally, he moves his body, in the sense that there is *some* description of the movement under which he knows that he makes it. Such descriptions are, to be sure, apt to be trivial and unrevealing; this is what ensures their existence. So, if I tie my shoelaces, here is a description of my movements: I move my body in just the way required to tie my shoelaces. Similarly, when I utter words, it is true that I am unable to describe what my tongue and mouth do, or to name the muscles I move. But I do not need the terminology of the speech therapist: what I do is move my mouth and muscles, as I know how to do, in just the way needed to produce the words I have in mind.

So there is after all no trouble in producing familiar and correct descriptions of my bodily movements, and these are the events that cause such further events as my shoelaces' being tied or the air's vibrating with my words. Of course, the describing trick has been turned by describing the actions as the movements with the right effects; but this does not show the trick has not been turned. What was needed was not a description that did not mention the effects, but a description that fitted the cause. There is, I conclude, nothing standing in the way of saying that our primitive actions, at least if we set aside such troublesome cases as mental acts, are bodily movements.

To return to the question whether the concept of action may be analyzed in terms of the concept of causality: what our discussion has shown is that we may concentrate on primitive actions. The ordinary notion of event-causality is useful in explaining how agency can spread from primitive actions to actions described in further ways, but it cannot in the same way explain the basic sense of agency. What we must ask, then, is whether there is another kind of causality, one that does not reduce to event-causality, an appeal to which will help us understand agency. We may call this kind of causality (following Thalberg) *agent-causality*.

Restricting ourselves, for the reason just given, to primitive actions, how well does the idea of agent-causality account for the relation between an agent and his action? There is this dilemma: either the causing by an agent of a primitive action is an event discrete from the primitive action, in which case we have problems about acts of the will or worse, or it is not a discrete event, in which case there seems no difference between saying someone caused a primitive action and saying he was the agent.

To take the first horn: suppose that causing a primitive

action (in the sense of agent-causality) does introduce an event separate from, and presumably prior to, the action. This prior event in turn must either be an action, or not. If an action, then the action we began with was not, contrary to our assumption, primitive. If not an action, then we have tried to explain agency by appeal to an even more obscure notion, that of a causing that is not a doing.

One is impaled on the second horn of the dilemma if one supposes that agent-causation does *not* introduce an event in addition to the primitive action. For then what more have we said when we say the agent caused the action than when we say he was the agent of the action? The concept of *cause* seems to play no role. We may fail to detect the vacuity of this suggestion because causality does, as we have noticed, enter conspicuously into accounts of agency; but where it does it is the garden-variety of causality, which sheds no light on the relation between the agent and his primitive actions.

We explain a broken window by saying that a brick broke it; what explanatory power the remark has derives from the fact that we may first expand the account of the cause to embrace an event, the movement of the brick, and we can then summon up evidence for the existence of a law connecting such events as motions of medium-sized rigid objects and the breaking of windows. The ordinary notion of cause is inseparable from this elementary form of explanation. But the concept of agent-causation lacks these features entirely. What distinguishes agent-causation from ordinary causation is that no expansion into a tale of two events is possible, and no law lurks. By the same token, nothing is explained. There seems no good reason, therefore, for using such expressions as "cause," "bring about," "make the case" to *illuminate* the relation between an agent and his act. I do not mean that there is anything wrong with such expressions – there are times when they come naturally in talk of agency. But I do not think that by introducing them we make any progress towards understanding agency and action.

Causality is central to the concept of agency, but it is ordinary causality between events that is relevant, and it concerns the effects and not the causes of actions (discounting, as before, the possibility of analyzing intention in terms of causality). One way to bring this out is by describing what Joel Feinberg calls the "accordion effect,"[9] which is an important feature of the language we use to describe actions. A man moves his finger, let us say intentionally, thus flicking the switch, causing a light to come on, the room to be illuminated, and a prowler to be alerted. This statement has the following entailments: the man flicked the switch, turned on the light, illuminated the room, and alerted the prowler. Some of these things he did intentionally, some not; beyond the finger movement, intention is irrelevant to the inferences, and even there it is required only in the sense that the movement must be intentional under some description. In brief, once he has done one thing (move a finger), each consequence presents us with a deed; an agent causes what his actions cause.[10]

The accordion effect will not reveal in what respect an act is intentional. If someone moves his mouth in such a way as to produce the words "your bat is on hackwards," thus

9 Joel Feinberg, "Action and Responsibility," in *Philosophy in America*, edited by Max Black (Ithaca, NY: Cornell University Press, 1965).
10 The formulation in this sentence is more accurate than some of my examples. Suppose Jones intentionally causes Smith intentionally to shoot Clifford to death. We certainly won't conclude that Jones shot Clifford, and we may or may not say that Jones killed Clifford. Still, my formulation is correct provided we can go from "Jones's action caused Clifford's death" to "Jones caused Clifford's death." There will, of course, be a conflict if we deny that both Jones and Smith (in our story) could be said to have caused Clifford's death, and at the same time affirm the transitivity of causality. We could, however, preserve the formula in the face of a denial that under the circumstances Jones could be said to have caused Clifford's death by saying that under the circumstances the transitivity of causality also breaks down. For further discussion of the issue, see H. L. A. Hart and A. M. Honoré, *Causation in the Law* (Oxford: The Clarendon Press, 1959); Joel Feinberg, "Causing Voluntary Actions," in *Metaphysics and Explanation*, edited by W. H. Capitan and D. D. Merrill (Pittsburgh: University of Pittsburgh Press, 1965); and J. E. Atwell, "The Accordion-Effect Thesis," *The Philosophical Quarterly*, 19 (1969), 337–342.

causing offence to his companion, the accordion effect applies, for we may say both that he spoke those words and that he offended his companion. Yet it is possible that he did not intend to move his mouth so as to produce those words, nor to produce them, nor to offend his companion. But the accordion effect is not applicable if there is no intention present. If the officer presses a button thinking it will ring a bell that summons a steward to bring him a cup of tea, but in fact it fires a torpedo that sinks the *Bismark*, then the officer sank the *Bismark*; but if he fell against the button because a wave upset his balance, then, though the consequences are the same, we will not count him as the agent.

The accordion effect is limited to agents. If Jones intentionally swings a bat that strikes a ball that hits and breaks a window, then Jones not only struck the ball but also broke the window. But we do not say that the bat, or even its movement, broke the window, though of course the movement of the bat caused the breakage. We do indeed allow that inanimate objects cause or bring about various things – in our example, the ball did break the window. However, this is not the accordion effect of agency, but only the ellipsis of event-causality. The ball broke the window – that is to say, its motion caused the breakage.

It seems therefore that we may take the accordion effect as a mark of agency. It is a way of inquiring whether an event is a case of agency to ask whether we can attribute its effects to a person. And on the other hand, whenever we say a person has done something where what we mention is clearly not a bodily movement, we have made him the agent not only of the mentioned event, but of some bodily movement that brought it about. In the case of bodily movements we sometimes have a brief way of mentioning a person and an event and yet of leaving open the question of whether he was the agent, as: Smith fell down.

The accordion effect is interesting because it shows that we treat the consequences of actions differently from the way in which we treat the consequences of other events. This shows that there is, after all, a fairly simple linguistic test that sometimes reveals that we take an event to be an action. But as a criterion it can hardly be counted as satisfactory: it works for some cases only, and of course it gives no clue as to what makes a primitive action an action.

At this point I abandon the search for an analysis of the concept of agency that does not appeal to intention, and turn to a related question that has come to the fore in the discussion of agent-causality and the accordion effect. The new question is what relation an agent has to those of his actions that are not primitive, those actions in describing which we go beyond mere movements of the body and dwell on the consequences, on what the agent has wrought in the world beyond his skin. Assuming that we understand agency in the case of primitive actions, how exactly are such actions related to the rest? The question I now raise may seem already to have been settled, but in fact it has not. What *is* clear is the relation between a primitive action, say moving one's finger in a certain way, and a consequence such as one's shoelaces being tied: it is the relation of event-causality. But this does not give a clear answer to the question of how the movement of the hands is related to the action of tying one's shoelaces, nor for that matter, to the question of how the action of tying one's shoelaces is related to one's shoelaces being tied. Or, to alter the example, if Brutus killed Caesar by stabbing him, what is the relation between these two actions, the relation expressed by the "by"? No doubt it is true that Brutus killed Caesar because the stabbing resulted in Caesar's death; but we still have that third event whose relations to the others are unclear, namely the killing itself.

It is natural to assume that the action whose mention includes mention of an outcome itself somehow includes that outcome. Thus Feinberg says that a man's action may be "squeezed down to a minimum or else stretched out" by the accordion effect. "He turned the key, he opened the door, he startled Smith, he killed Smith – all of these are things we might say that Jones *did* with one identical set of bodily movements," Feinberg tells us. It is just this relation of "doing with" or "doing by" in which we are interested. Feinberg continues: "We can, if we wish, puff out an action to include an effect."[11] Puffing out, squeezing down, stretching out sound like operations performed on one and the same event; yet if, as seems clear, these operations change the time span of the event, then it cannot be one and the same event: on Feinberg's theory, the action of opening the door cannot be identical with the action of startling Smith. That this is Feinberg's view comes out more clearly in his distinction between simple and causally complex acts. Simple acts are those which require us to do nothing else (we have been calling these primitive actions); causally complex acts, such as opening or shutting a door, or startling, or killing someone, require us to do *something else* first, as a means.[12] Thus Feinberg says, "In order to open a door, we must first do something else which will *cause* the door to open; but to move one's finger one simply moves it – no prior causal activity is required."[13] He also talks of "causally connected sequences of acts."

The idea that opening a door requires prior causal activity, a movement that causes the door to open, is not Feinberg's alone. He quotes J. L. Austin in the same vein: "... a single term descriptive of what he did may be made to cover either a smaller or a larger stretch of events, those excluded by the narrower description being then called 'consequences' or 'results' or 'effects' or the like of his act."[14] Arthur Danto has drawn the distinction, in several articles, between "basic acts," such as moving a hand, and other acts that are caused by the basic acts, such as moving a stone.[15]

---

11 Feinberg, "Action and Responsibility," p. 146. I am concerned with an issue that is not central in Feinberg's excellent paper. Even if my *caveats* are justified, his thesis is not seriously affected.
12 *Ibid.*, p. 145.
13 *Ibid.*, p. 147.
14 Austin, "A Plea for Excuses," p. 145.
15 Arthur Danto, "What We Can Do," *Journal of Philosophy*, 60 (1963),

It seems to me that this conception of actions and their consequences contains several closely related but quite fundamental confusions. It is a mistake to think that when I close the door of my own free will *anyone* normally causes me to do it, even myself, or that any prior or other action of mine causes me to close the door. What my action causes is the closing of the door. So the second error is to confuse what my action of moving my hand does cause – the closing of the door – with something utterly different – my action of closing the door. And the third mistake, which is forced by the others, is to suppose that when I close the door by moving my hand, I perform two numerically distinct actions (as I would have to if one were needed to cause the other). In the rest of this paper I develop these points.[16]

There is more than a hint of conflict between two incompatible ideas in Austin and Feinberg. As we noticed before, Feinberg shows some inclination to treat moving one's hand and opening the door (and startling Smith, etc.) as one and the same action, which is somehow stretched out or contracted; but he also says things that seem to contradict this, especially when he claims that one must first do something else to cause the door to open in order to open the door. The same strain is noticeable in Austin's pronouncement, for he speaks of different terms descriptive of *what the man did* – apparently one and the same thing – but the terms "cover"

435–445; "Basic Actions," *American Philosophical Quarterly*, 2 (1965), 141–148; "Freedom and Forbearance," in *Freedom and Determinism*. Chisholm endorses the distinction in "Freedom and Action," p. 39.

16 Danto's view that if I close the door by moving my hand, my action of closing the door is caused by my moving my hand, has been ably criticized by Myles Brand, "Danto on Basic Actions," *Noûs*, 2 (1968), 187–190; Frederick Stoutland, "Basic Actions and Causality," *Journal of Philosophy*, 65 (1968), 467–475; Wilfrid Sellars, "Metaphysics and the Concept of a Person," in *The Logical Way of Doing Things*, edited by Karel Lambert (New Haven: Yale University Press, 1969).

My target is more general: I want to oppose any view that implies that if I do A by doing B then my doing A and my doing B must be numerically distinct.

smaller or larger stretches of events. Events that cover different stretches cannot be identical.[17]

There are, I think, insuperable difficulties that stand in the way of considering these various actions, the primitive actions like moving a hand, and the actions in describing which we refer to the consequences, as numerically distinct.

It is evident that the relation between the queen's moving her hand in such a way as to pour poison in the king's ear, and her killing him, cannot be the relation of event-causality. If it were, we would have to say the queen caused herself to kill the king. This is not the same as saying the queen brought it about, or made it the case, that she killed the king; these locutions, while strained, do not seem clearly wrong, for it is not clear that they mean anything more than that the queen brought herself to kill the king. But then the locutions cannot be causal in the required sense. For suppose that by moving her hand the queen caused herself to kill the king. Then we could ask how she did this causing. The only answer I can imagine is that she did it by moving her hand in that way. But this movement was by itself enough to cause the death of the king – there was no point to a further action on the part of the queen. Nor is there any reason (unless we add to the story in an irrelevant way) why the queen should have wanted to cause herself to kill the king. What she wanted to do was kill the king – that is, do something that would cause his death. Is it not absurd to suppose that, after the queen has moved her hand in such a way as to cause the king's death, any deed remains for her to do or to complete? She has done her work; it only remains for the poison to do its.

It will not help to think of killing as an action that begins when the movement of the hand takes place but ends later. For once again, when we inquire into the relation between these events, the answer must be that the killing consists of

17 There is further discussion of these issues in my "The Individuation of Events," in *Essays in Honor of Carl G. Hempel*, edited by Nicholas Rescher *et al.* (Dordrecht: D. Reidel, 1970).

the hand movement and one of its consequences. We can put them together this way because the movement of the hand caused the death. But then, in moving her hand, the queen was doing something that caused the death of the king. These are two descriptions of the same event – the queen moved her hand in that way; she did something that caused the death of the king. (Or to put it, as I would rather, in terms of a definite description: The moving of her hand by the queen on that occasion was identical with her doing something that caused the death of the king.) Doing something that causes a death is identical with causing a death. But there is no distinction to be made between causing the death of a person and killing him.[18] It follows that what we thought was a more attenuated event – the killing – took no more time, and did not differ from, the movement of the hand.

The idea that under the assumed circumstances killing a person differs from moving one's hand in a certain way springs from a confusion between a feature of the description of an event and a feature of the event itself. The mistake consists in thinking that when the description of an event is made to include reference to a consequence, then the consequence itself is included in the described event. The accordion, which remains the same through the squeezing and stretching, is the action; the changes are in aspects described, or descriptions of the event. There are, in fact, a great many tunes we can play on the accordion. We could start with "The queen moved her hand" and pull to the right by adding "thus causing the vial to empty into the king's ear"; and now another tug, "thus causing the poison to enter the body of the king"; and finally (if we have had enough – for the possibilities for expansion are without clear limit), "thus causing the king to die." This expression can be shortened in many ways, into the centre, the left, or the right

18 See footnote 10. The argument goes through if the claim of this sentence is weakened by adding "in the case where a person is killed by doing something that causes his death."

components, or any combination. For some examples: "The queen moved her hand thus causing the death of the king" (the two ends); or, "The queen killed the king" (collapse to the right); or "The queen emptied the vial into the king's ear" (the centre). There is another way to pull the instrument out, too: we could *start* with "The queen killed the king," adding "by pouring poison in his ear," and so on – addition to the left. Many of these expressions are equivalent: for example, "The queen killed the king by pouring poison in his ear" and "The queen poured poison in the king's ear thus causing his death." And obviously the longer descriptions entail many of the shorter ones.

But this welter of related descriptions corresponds to a single descriptum – this is the conclusion on which our considerations all converge.[19] When we infer that he stopped his car from the fact that by pressing a pedal a man caused his automobile to come to a stop, we do not transfer agency from one event to another, or infer that the man was agent not only of one action but of two. We may indeed extend responsibility or liability for an action to responsibility or liability for its consequences, but this we do, not by saddling the agent with a new action, but by pointing out that his original action had those results.

We must conclude, perhaps with a shock of surprise, that our primitive actions, the ones we do not do by doing something else, mere movements of the body – these are all the actions there are. We never do more than move our bodies: the rest is up to nature.

This doctrine, while not quite as bad as the bad old doctrine that all we ever do is will things to happen, or set ourselves to act, may seem to share some of the same disadvantages. Let me briefly indicate why I do not think that this is so.

---

19 This conclusion is not new. It was clearly stated by G. E. M. Anscombe, *Intention* (Oxford: Blackwell, 1959), pp. 37–47. I followed suit in "Actions, Reasons, and Causes."

First, it will be said that some actions require that we do others in order to bring them off, and so cannot be primitive: for example, before I can hit the bull's eye, I must load and raise my gun, then aim and pull the trigger. Of course I do not deny we must prepare the way for some actions by performing others. The criticism holds only if this shows some actions are not primitive. In the present example, the challenge is to demonstrate that hitting the bull's eye is a primitive action. And this it is, according to the argument I have given; for hitting the bull's eye is no more than doing something that causes the bull's eye to be hit, and this, given the right conditions, including a weapon, I can do by holding my arms in a certain position and moving my trigger finger.

Second, it is often said that primitive actions are distinguished by the fact that we know, perhaps without need of observation or evidence, that we are performing them, while this is not a feature of such further events as hitting a bull's eye. But of course we can know that a certain event is taking place when it is described in one way and not know that it is taking place when described in another. Even when we are doing something intentionally, we may not know that we are doing it; this is even more obviously true of actions when described in terms of their unintended begettings.

Finally, it may seem a difficulty that primitive actions do not accommodate the concept of trying, for primitive actions are ones we just do – nothing can stand in the way, so to speak. But surely, the critic will say, there are some things we must strive to do (like hit the bull's eye). Once more the same sort of answer serves. Trying to do one thing may be simply doing another. I try to turn on the light by flicking the switch, but I simply flick the switch. Or perhaps even that is, on occasion, an attempt. Still, the attempt consists of something I can do without trying; just move my hand, perhaps.

The same fact underlies the last two answers: being attempted and being known to occur are not characteristics of events, but of events as described or conceived in one way or another. It is this fact too that explains why we may be limited, in our actions, to mere movements of our bodies, and yet may be capable, for better or for worse, of building dams, stemming floods, murdering one another, or, from time to time, hitting the bull's eye.

We may now return to the question of the relation between an agent and his action. The negative result we have reached is this: the notion of cause has nothing directly to do with this relation. Knowledge that an action *a* has a certain upshot allows us to describe the agent as the cause of that upshot, but this is merely a convenient way of redescribing *a*, and of *it*, as we have seen, there is no point in saying that he is the cause. Causality allows us to redescribe actions in ways we cannot redescribe other events; this fact is a mark of actions, but yields no analysis of agency.

To say that all actions are primitive actions is merely to acknowledge, perhaps in a misleading way, the fact that the concept of being primitive, like the concept of being intentional, is intensional, and so cannot mark out a *class* of actions. If an event is an action, then under some description(s) it is primitive, and under some description(s) it is intentional. This explains why we were frustrated in the attempt to assume a basic concept of agency as applied to primitive actions and extend it to further actions defined in terms of the consequences of primitive actions: the attempt fails because there are no further actions, only further descriptions.

The collapse of all actions into the primitive, which is marked in syntax by the accordion effect, leads to a vast simplification of the problem of agency, for it shows that there is a relation between a person and an event, when it is his action, that is independent of how the terms of the relation are described. On the other hand, we have discovered no analysis of this relation that does not appeal to the concept of intention. Whether intention can be understood in terms of more basic or simpler ideas is a question with which I have not tried to cope in this paper.

B

Comments

BY JAMES CORNMAN

There are several very interesting points that Professor Davidson makes in his paper, and, although I shall not discuss them all in detail, I would at least like to highlight some of them with a few comments. In order of appearance they are as follows. First, Davidson defines, or at least provides necessary and sufficient conditions for, "Person P is the agent of event a" in terms of P's intentions and descriptions of a. I shall discuss this point in detail and try to show that, as I understand Davidson's views, he faces objections to both the "if" and the "only if" parts of his definition.

Second, Davidson hints in passing (p. 9) that the difference between a situation in which someone raises his arm and one in which his arm merely goes up is not the occurrence of an act of will in the former but not the latter case, but rather is the occurrence in the former of a certain kind of cause of his arm going up, such as a desire to get something from a shelf. This point opens up a whole fascinating and relatively untapped area, but I can here make only a few sketchy remarks. I tend to agree with Davidson that the difference in the two situations is a difference in cause. Where I am more skeptical is in agreeing with Davidson's classification of such differentiating causes as desires (p. 9). I tend more to let the classification be determined by scientists, leaving open the question of whether they classify the relevant event as a brain process, or a desire, or perhaps some postulated theoretical entity that fits neither of those two classifications.

Third, Davidson makes the most interesting point that, although the ordinary concept of event-causality is needed for a satisfactory account of agency, agent-causality conceived as something irreducibly different from event-causation is of no value for such an account. He states a dilemma to show this (p. 13). We can reconstruct it as follows: either the event of P causing a is different from the action of P being agent of a or it is not. If it is different, then to avoid an infinite regress the event of P causing a is not an action of P. Thus this alternative posits an event that accompanies every action but which is distinct from every action. Davidson sees no reason to do this, for that would be explaining agency by "an even more obscure notion, that of a causing that is not a doing" (p. 13). If the event and the action are identical, however, Davidson finds no gain over merely saying that P is the agent of a, and thus positing agent-causality is again unjustified. I have doubts about both horns of the dilemma. First, if my sketchy comments on the second point are roughly correct, there may be a distinguishing kind of cause, whether desire, brain process, or whatever, that accompanies all cases of action (because it causes the event) but which is itself not an action. This cause might be a desire, as Davidson claims, but it might also be an event of desiring or even a brain event. If either of the latter is correct, then it could be argued that agent-causation is reducible to regular, "unobscure" event-causation, because my causing an event would be identical with some desiring or some brain event causing the event. But if, as Davidson claims, it is a desire that causes the event, then, I should think, because a desire is not an event, agent-causation is not reducible to event-causation. Nor would it be reducible, if, to explain the particular events of which people are agents, scientists postulated an ego or some other kind of subject, a subject which, for example, so affected brain events that in, and only in, such cases would they cause those particular bodily events. But even so, it is not clear that this kind of causing is doomed to obscurity. It might be explicated scientifically.

Concerning the second horn of the dilemma, Davidson is correct in saying that if one takes this horn one has neither explained nor helpfully analyzed P being the agent of a merely by saying that P causes a, but this does not show that there is no need for agency-causation as irreducibly different from event-causation. Nor does it preclude that such a causal concept might come to be part of a respectable scientific explanatory theory. At most it shows that there is no need for the three relations: P is the agent cause of a, e is event cause of a, and P is the agent of a. On this view of agency we do not need both the first and third relations, but Davidson has not shown that we do not need at least one. And if we do need one, then no matter which it is, someone who grasps the second horn could claim that that relation is indeed agent-causation. On my part I think the most we should say here is that we *may* need more than mere event-causation to explain agency, but also we may not. The decision about whether there is such a need or not does not seem to be purely a philosophical decision.

Davidson's fourth point is also controversial and, on the face of it, blatantly false. He says that "our primitive actions, the ones we do not do by doing something else, mere movements of the body – these are all the actions there are" (p. 23). This claim seems clearly false because people do such actions as sinking ships, and, it seems clear, such actions are not "mere movements of the body." But this is where Davidson disagrees. His view is that all actions such as sinking ships are identical with the actions of causing ships to sink, and all actions of causing ships to sink are identical with primitive actions, that is, with bodily movements. Now there may be something wrong here, but if there is, it is not blatant. Indeed the issues here are rather subtle, too subtle to grasp easily. However, because one of the problems that arises for Davidson in adopting his "if and only if" definition of "P is the agent of event a" arises because of his reduction of all actions to bodily movements, I shall defer discussion of this reduction until later when more details of his view are made available.

DEFINITION OF "*P* IS THE AGENT OF EVENT *a*"

Toward the beginning of his discussion of agency, Davidson concludes that perhaps "being intentional is the relevant distinguishing mark" of agency (p. 5). But he points out that it can be true to say that an event is done intentionally when described in one way, but false when described in another way. Thus he first states his mark of agency in the following way: "A man is the agent of an act if what he does can be described under an aspect that makes it intentional" (p. 7). This is less than clear, but I think it can be clarified and seen to be true. Davidson, himself, clarifies it soon after in an "if and only if" definition which provides, thereby, not only a mark of agency but also a mark of the absence of agency. He says: "A person is the agent of an event if and only if there is a description of what he did that makes true a sentence that says that he did it intentionally" (p. 7). I shall assume this is Davidson's final statement and shall try to do four things: first, clarify it symbolically; second, restate it without quantification over descriptions; third, cast doubt on intentionality as a necessary condition of agency; and fourth, cast doubt on conjoining the true claim that being intentional is a sufficient condition of agency with other claims Davidson makes in his paper.

The first two tasks can be completed quickly. We can avoid talk of being "under aspects," of descriptions *making* sentences true, and of sentences *saying* things by using the following symbolism:

D1   *P* is the agent of event *a* $\equiv$ $(\exists x)$ $(Dxa \cdot$ "*P* did *y* intentionally" is true if *x* is substituted for "*y*"),

where $Dxa = x$ is a description of *a*. This I think is clear enough, but I should like also to unpack "*P* did *y* intentionally" somewhat. I shall interpret it as "*P* did *y* with the intention of doing *y*." This makes clearer which conditions a description must fulfil as a value of the variable "*y*" in order to meet Davidson's marks of agency and non-agency.

One bothersome thing about Davidson's definition is that it quantifies over descriptions. Not only might it be preferred not to quantify over such entities unless it is necessary, but also it can be doubted that a person is an agent of an event only if there is some description to describe it. It seems at least possible that people be agents and there be no language, and thus no descriptions. I know that some people would think this is not possible, and it surely is a debatable point. Rather than argue it here, however, I shall attempt to restate Davidson's definition in such a way that only events are quantified over – something Davidson thinks is necessary anyway. If my proposal succeeds, then, because it avoids the debate about quantification over descriptions, we can disagree with Davidson when he claims that "to do better [than his formulation] would require a semantic analysis of sentences about propositional attitudes" (p. 7).

In Davidson's definition, descriptions of the event *a* are referred to, and it is only required that there be some description of *a* that results in a true sentence when substituted in "*P* did *y* intentionally." But why can we not talk in the material mode rather than the formal mode and refer to some event that is identical with *a* rather than to some descriptions of *a*? What we would get is:

D2   *P* is the agent of event $a \equiv (\exists x)$ $(Ex \cdot P$ did x intentionally $\cdot x = a)$,

where $Ex = x$ is an event. We might go one step further if we interpret "*P* did *x* intentionally" in the way I have suggested, that is, as "*P* did *x* with the intention of doing *x*." We might, then, replace Davidson's definition with:

D3   *P* is the agent of event $a \equiv (\exists x)$ $(Ex \cdot P$ did a with the intention of doing x)

It certainly seems that the definiens of 1 entails the definiens of 2, but the converse seems false because the first entails that there be descriptions and the second seems not to. The only objection to the entailment would arise if someone were to show that a conjunction of sentences, such as " '*e*' is a description of *a*," and " '*P* did *e*' is true," do not entail that *e* = *a*. And although this objection might be developed (depending, among other things, on how "a description of" is interpreted), I shall not do so here, because I do not think that Davidson makes any of his points depend on it. We can also say that on my interpretation of "*P* did *x* intentionally" both the definiens of 1 and 2 entail that of 3, because substitution of extensionally equivalent terms for the *first* occurrence of *x* in "*P* did *x* with the intention of doing *x*" is *salva veritate*. But the definiens of 3 seems not to entail that of 1 because of the latter's quantification over descriptions; nor does it entail the definiens of 2 because the latter but not the former entails that *x* = *a*.

One thing is clear about these three different proposals: that 3 commits one to the least and, it seems, 1 commits him to the most. This is part of the reason why I, at the moment at least, prefer 3. However, I have not had time to go into the matter in sufficient detail. Consequently I shall say no more about 3, but from here on will work with 1 and 2, ignoring the difference about quantification over descriptions.

EXAMINATION OF INTENTIONALITY AS A NECESSARY CONDITION OF AGENCY

Although Davidson began by looking for a mark of agency, we have seen he has also given us a mark of non-agency, that is, a necessary condition of agency. He claims that a person *P* is the agent of an event *a* only if there is some description, *x*, of *a* such that "*P* did *x* intentionally" is true. It seems to me that although a person *P* is the agent of an event *a* only if *P* did *a*, it is not required that he intentionally did some event that is identical with *a*. Part of my problem is that I have difficulty distinguishing between being the agent of an event and doing it. Of course, if there is no difference then Davidson's definition is of little value. But even assuming there is a difference, I think there are cases of agency where there is no description, x, of the event such that "P did x intentionally" is true. The clearest class of cases are those of negligence, where a man is the agent of an event, although he intended to do nothing whatsoever. The man who starts a forest fire by absent-mindedly dropping a lighted match or by flipping away a cigarette out of habit often has no intention at the time at all. He may not intend to drop the match, throw it away, or anything else. He just failed to think about or pay any attention to what he was doing. He may, of course, sometimes have some intention at the time, but it may be irrelevant to what he did. He may be intending to cut down a tree, for example, and his concentration on that might explain his negligence. In such cases I would claim that the person is the agent of the event of the forest fire beginning, and that there is no description, x, of that event such that "He did x intentionally" is true. Therefore, I conclude that intentionality as stated in definition 1, and also in 2 and 3, is not a necessary condition of agency, at least as I understand agency. Consequently all three definitions fail.

EXAMINATION OF INTENTIONALITY AS A SUFFICIENT CONDITION OF AGENCY

Nothing we have said shows that intentionality is not a sufficient condition of agency. Indeed, as stated in definition 3, I think it is. However, although I also think that as stated in definition 1, intentionality is sufficient for agency, I find that when this half of 1 is conjoined with other claims by Davidson, implausible conclusions result. There is, in short, a problem internal to Davidson's theory of agency.

The problem arises from Davidson's way of arguing for

his claim that all human actions, even those described in terms relating to the consequences of bodily movements, are identical with primitive actions which are bodily movements. He argues by way of example. He considers the case of the queen killing the king by pouring poison in his ear. Davidson claims that the event of the queen killing the king is identical with the event of the movement of her hand in pouring the poison in his ear. What he says is:

> But then in moving her hand, the queen was doing something that caused the death of the king. These are two descriptions of the same event – the queen moved her hand in that way; she did something that caused the death of the king. (Or to put it, as I would rather, in terms of definite descriptions: The moving of her hand by the queen was identical with her doing something that caused the death of the king.) Doing something that causes a death is identical with causing a death. But there is no distinction to be made between causing the death of a person and killing him. It follows that what we thought was a more attenuated event – the killing – took no more time, and did not differ from, the movement of the hand (p. 22).

On the assumption that Davidson uses this example to illustrate a more general argument, it would seem that we can state his argument as follows:

1 Doing something that causes a death is identical with causing a death.
2 There is no distinction between causing the death of a person and killing him.

Therefore,

3 Doing something that causes the death of a person is identical with killing him.
4 All doings of something that causes a death are bodily movements.

Therefore,

5 All killings of persons (and any other actions) are bodily movements.

If we take these three premisses that I have extracted from
Davidson's argument we can combine them with other
plausible premisses to derive conclusions that are counter-
examples to Davidson's version of intentionality as a mark of
agency. Consider the case of Jones who wires a switch
incorrectly because he was given an incorrect wiring diagram,
and, as a result, a moon rocket explodes on take-off, killing
its crew. He, by wiring the switch the way he did – something
he did intentionally, did something that caused the death of
the crew. But I should think that we would not say that he
performed the action of killing them nor that he was the
agent of their dying. If, however, we conjoin the preceding
with Davidson's premiss 4 we can conclude that this doing
of something that caused death of the crew is one of Jones's
bodily movements. Clearly it must be those movements that
can be described by talking of his wiring the switch intentionally. Furthermore, by Davidson's premisses 1 and 2, we
can conclude that his doing something that caused the death
of the crew is identical with killing them. Thus Jones's killing
the crew is the same as the bodily movements Jones performed intentionally. This meets the antecedent of Davidson's
intentionality mark of agency. But if human agency is to be
more than the agency expressed in "The rocket explosion
killed the crew," then Jones was not *the* agent, nor even *an*
agent of the crew's death. Thus the consequent is not met.
We have found a counterexample to Davidson's intentionality
mark of agency using Davidson's own statements.

Fortunately, Davidson can avoid this problem by modifying
premiss 2 in a way that does not affect his argument justifying
5. The counterexample works only if Davidson accepts:

2A Causing the death of someone is killing him.

This is entailed by 2, i.e., there is no distinction between causing the death of a person and killing him. But the counterexample does not work if Davidson states merely:

2B Killing someone is causing his death.

The counterexample requires that we infer from doing something that causes death to causing death and then, via 2A, to killing the person. But 2A – and therefore 2 – is false, as the rocket example illustrates. However, 2B, which I think is true, is all Davidson's argument needs. Let me, then, state and then examine Davidson's argument when put in a form using 2B and a reasonable revision of 1.

2B Killing someone is causing his death.
1A Causing someone's death is doing something that causes his death.

Therefore,

3A Killing someone is doing something that causes his death.|
4 All doings of something that causes a death are bodily movements.

Therefore,

5 All killings of someone are bodily movements.

EXAMINATION OF REVISED FORM
OF DAVIDSON'S ARGUMENT

I think we can agree that premisses 1A and 2B are true. We can also agree that the argument is valid when the ambiguous phrase "killings of someone" in conclusion 5 is interpreted in one way, although it is invalid when interpreted differently. The phrase "a killing," just like the phrase "an action," can mean either a doing, i.e., activity of someone, or the object of the activity (perhaps what Davidson calls the "upshot") (p. 25). The latter, whether a killing of a person, or a sinking

of a ship, or whatever, is often not a bodily movement even
if the activities of killing, sinking, etc. are. They occur when
someone dies or a ship sinks and thus often after the bodily
movements that cause them. I mention this meaning of
"action," etc., only to point out that we do distinguish among
these "upshot" actions of a person and do not reduce them
to bodily movements. But since for the activity sense of
"killing" the argument is valid, let us concentrate on the
argument with "killing" so interpreted.

My doubts about the argument centre on premiss 4 even
once we interpret bodily movements broadly, as Davidson
suggests (p. 11), to include motionless actions and mental
acts. Perhaps we should coin a term such as "person-event"
rather than use "bodily movement" in order to avoid confusion. But, even so, there is the obvious objection that the
blowing up of the rocket by Jones, which is doing something
that causes the crew's death, is not one of Jones's bodily
movements. How is Davidson to refute this objection? He
certainly cannot merely assume it is true because the very
doubts one has about his argument's conclusion apply here
also. If his conclusion about killing someone needs to be
established, then so also would a parallel claim about blowing
up things.

I do not know how Davidson might try to establish premiss 4. What I wish to do in ending this paper, is to state an
argument that purports to disprove 4 with the hope that this
will stimulate a discussion that will clarify the issues sur-
rounding the question of whether all killings, and indeed all
actions of any kind, are, as Davidson claims, bodily
movements.

AN ARGUMENT TO DISPROVE PREMISS 4

The argument I shall present centres on Davidson's concept
of primitive action. I shall use two premisses derived from

what he says about such actions and another one which, on the face of it, seems to be true. The argument is as follows:

6 If a doing of something that causes a death is also a bodily movement, then it is a primitive action.
7 All primitive actions are actions which persons do not do by doing something else (see p. 19 and p. 22).
8 Some doings of something that causes a death are actions which persons do by doing something else.

Therefore,

9 Some doings of something that causes a death are not bodily movements, i.e., premiss 4 is false.

Incidentally, a parallel argument would apply to Davidson's conclusion, 5. Premiss 7 is explicitly stated by Davidson and I think it is true. As I understand the relationship between bodily movements and primitive actions that Davidson espouses, I think he would also agree to 6. And, so far as I can see, it is true. Premiss 8 also appears to be true. It surely seems true of some doings that cause a death (such as someone's blowing up of a rocket), that the person does something else to accomplish the death (such as pushing a button or a dynamite plunger). I suspect that it is here that Davidson will disagree, but it is not clear to me what his reasons for this might be.

2 / On the Logic of Intentional Action

Roderick Chisholm

I

I shall consider certain concepts that seem to me essential for understanding action and intention; I shall attempt to show how they may be explicated in terms of the concept of causation and one other undefined concept; I shall make some suggestions about the logic of this locution, a logic that is similar in fundamental respects to that of necessity and possibility; and then I shall apply these considerations to a number of philosophical questions pertaining to the nature of action.[1]

The philosophical background of this paper may be suggested by the following general theses: that persons, or selves, are substantival, concrete things, in the strictest sense of the term "thing"; that there *are* states of affairs, some of which obtain and some of which do not obtain; that persons, like states of affairs, may cause states of affairs to obtain; and therefore that there is a valid distinction between what Professor Broad has called "occurrent causation" (a set of states of affairs causing a state of affairs to obtain) and what

[1] I have discussed some of these questions in "Some Puzzles about Agency," in *The Logical Way of Doing Things: Philosophical Essays in Honor of Henry S. Leonard*, edited by Karel Lambert (New Haven: Yale University Press, 1969); in "Freedom and Action," in *Freedom and Determinism*, edited by Keith Lehrer (New York: Random House, 1966); and in "The Descriptive Element in the Concept of Action," *Journal of Philosophy*, 61 (1964), 613–625. The system of concepts that is set forth in the present paper is an improvement over those that were set forth earlier.

he has called "non-occurrent causation" (a person causing a state of affairs to obtain).[2] The topic of the present paper, then, is "non-occurrent causation" in so far as it is intentional and teleological – a man causing certain states of affairs to obtain in the endeavour to cause certain (possibly other) states of affairs to obtain.

II

I shall first summarize very briefly and dogmatically, the ontology of "states of affairs" that is here presupposed.

For every well-formed sentence, there is a corresponding gerundive expression. Thus for "Socrates is mortal" there is "Socrates being mortal" as well as "It being the case that Socrates is mortal"; and for "Socrates is mortal and all swans are white," there is "Socrates being mortal and all swans being white" as well as "It being the case that Socrates is mortal and all swans are white." The gerundives of well-formed sentences may be said to designate states of affairs.

States of affairs are analogous to sentences in that they may be compound or non-compound (and if compound, then negative, or conjunctive, or disjunctive, and so on) and in that they may be said to entail (contain or have as parts) other states of affairs. States of affairs are of two sorts – those that obtain and those that do not obtain. Hence if a well-formed sentence is true, then the state of affairs that is designated by its corresponding gerundive is one that obtains; but if a well-formed sentence is false, then the state of affairs that is designated by its corresponding gerundive is one that does not obtain. And so we say that there *are* states of affairs, some of which obtain and some of which do not obtain. In place

2 See "Determinism, Indeterminism, and Libertarianism," in C. D. Broad, *Ethics and the History of Philosophy* (London: Routledge & Kegan Paul, 1952). Compare C. A. Campbell, "Is 'Free Will' a Pseudo-Problem?" *Mind*, 60 (1951), 441–465; and Joseph Rickaby, *Free Will and Four English Philosophers* (London: Burns & Oates, 1906).

of "obtains," we may say "takes place," or "occurs," or "is actual," or even "exists" (but if we use "exists," we should say "There *are* states of affairs that do not exist" and not "There *exist* states of affairs that do not exist"). "Facts," in at least one of its uses, refers to states of affairs that exist, or obtain.[3]

States of affairs, moreover, may be related to each other temporally. Thus one state of affairs may obtain *before* another state of affairs obtains. We may even say, somewhat paradoxically, that a state of affairs may obtain before itself. A man dying, for example, is a state of affairs that will obtain today and then obtain again tomorrow. We may assume, however, that when a man dying does thus occur before itself, it is then a part of a larger state of affairs (say, Jones's dying) which includes as well as precedes a man dying (Jones's dying, say, precedes Smith's dying) and which does *not* precede itself. More generally, we may assume that, for every state of affairs p, if p obtains, then there obtains a state of affairs q of the following sort: q entails (or contains) p, q and p are contemporaneous (neither begins before, nor lasts after, the other), and q does not precede itself. If we say that an "individual state of affairs" is a state of affairs that obtains and does not precede itself, then we may say that every state of affairs that obtains is part of (is entailed by) a certain individual state of affairs contemporaneous with it.[4]

3 Frege said, "A fact is a thought that is true." I believe it is accurate to say that he used "thought [Gedanke]" as we are using "state of affairs" and that he used "is true" as we are using "obtains." See G. Frege, "The Thought: A Logical Inquiry," as translated in *Mind*, 65 (1956), 289–311; the quotation is on p. 307. I believe it is also accurate to say that Russell once used "proposition" as we are now using "state of affairs," and "is true" and "is false" in application to what he called "propositions" as we are now using "obtains" and "does not obtain." See for example his "Meinong's Theory of Complexes and Assumptions," *Mind*, 13 (1904), 204–219, 336–354, and 509–524. Meinong's term for "state of affairs" was "*Objektive*"; see *Über Annahmen*, 2nd ed. (Leipzig: Johann Ambrosius Barth, 1910), Ch. 3. The present use of "state of affairs" is the same as that of C. I. Lewis in *An Analysis of Knowledge and Valuation* (La Salle, Ill.: Open Court, 1946), Ch. 3.
4 But we do not assume that, in *addition* to states of affairs, there is still

If we use "individual state of affairs" in this way, we should resist the temptation to say such things as that the inauguration of Mr. Johnson's successor and the inauguration of Mr. Nixon are "the same individual state of affairs." For they are different states of affairs. The inauguration of Mr. Johnson's successor, for example, entails, or has as a part, there being a Mr. Johnson and Mr. Johnson having a successor, but the inauguration of Mr. Nixon does not. (Talk about states of affairs, therefore, requires us to make use of contexts that are referentially opaque: from the fact that the *F* is identical with the *G*, we may not infer that whatever may be truly said about that state of affairs which is the *F* being *H* may also be said about that state of affairs which is the *G* being *H*.) We could, of course, *give* a use to such expressions as "The inauguration of Mr. Johnson's successor and the inauguration of Mr. Nixon constitute one and the same individual state of affairs" without going beyond our present ontology. One such use may be suggested by this formula: "The *F*'s being *H constitutes the same individual state of affairs* as does the *G*'s being *H*, if and only if, the *F* is *H* and is identical with the *G*." Hence, when it is convenient, we may say of two different states of affairs that they constitute one and the same individual state of affairs. But such talk must not mislead us into supposing that any two such states of affairs are identical with each other.[5]

another sort of entity that might be called an "event." We do not assume that there are those things that C. I. Lewis, *An Analysis of Knowledge and Valuation*, called "Whiteheadian events" or "spacetime slabs of reality," or that events are entities "in" which states of affairs might be "exemplified," or that they are in any clear sense "concrete," "particular," or "individual." Nor do we assume, with Lewis, that actual states of affairs "characterize" a certain entity, viz., "the actual world."

5 The ontology presupposed by the present paper, therefore, is quite different from that which is presupposed by Donald Davidson's account of agency; see his contribution to the present volume as well as his "The Logical Form of Action Sentences," in *The Logic of Decision and Action*, edited by Nicholas Rescher (Pittsburgh: The University of Pittsburgh Press, 1966). I believe that Davidson would say that there is a particular or concrete event which is the inauguration

I assume further that the familiar laws of propositional logic may be construed as laws pertaining to certain relations that hold necessarily among states of affairs. I also assume that states of affairs are related by "physical necessity." In other words, we may say of some states of affairs (e.g., no headless person having a head) that it is *logically necessary* that those states of affairs obtain; and we may say of some states of affairs (e.g., no headless person being alive) that it is *physically necessary* that those states of affairs obtain or, alternatively put, that it is a *law of nature* that those states of affairs obtain. I believe that this concept of a law of nature is essential to the analysis of "occurrent causation" – one state of affairs contributing causally to the occurrence of another state of affairs. For to say that one state of affairs contributes causally to the occurrence of a second is to say, in part, that the one is a member of a set of states of affairs constituting a sufficient causal condition for the occurrence of the second; and this is to say, in turn, that it is a law of nature that if the members of the set of states of affairs obtain then the second state of affairs will also obtain.

And I assume, finally, that states of affairs may be objects of our intentional attitudes. Witness: "There is something that both Smith and Jones wanted very much to happen and that they both strove hard to bring about. Namely? Senator McCarthy being elected President."

Now we may turn to intentional action.

III

Consider the statement, "He made the chickens fly in the endeavour to arouse his friend." As it would ordinarily be

of Mr. Johnson's successor and that this is identical with that particular or concrete event which is the inauguration of Mr. Nixon. He attempts to explicate human action by reference to such particular or concrete events and *without* reference to states of affairs, as the latter are here understood.

interpreted, the statement implies not only that the chickens flew, but also that the person referred to contributed causally to their flying; he brought about something which was part of the cause of their flying. It implies further that he had the purpose of arousing his friend and that he did something in order to realize or fulfil that purpose. But the statement does not imply that he was successful and therefore it does not imply that he did arouse his friend. Does it imply that he made the chickens fly *for the purpose* of arousing his friend?

Let us note two rather different situations in which our statement might be asserted. In the one case, the agent believes that by making the chickens fly he will create a disturbance that is sufficiently noisy to arouse his friend. If he does thus make the chickens fly in the endeavour to arouse his friend, then we may also say that he did so *for the purpose* of arousing his friend. But our original may also be asserted in a somewhat different situation.

Suppose the agent thought that by blowing his horn he would make a noise and that the noise would be loud enough to arouse his friend. Suppose he then blew his horn for the purpose of arousing his friend and, in so doing, he inadvertently aroused the chickens and thereby made them fly. In a situation of this sort, our original statement, "He made the chickens fly for the purpose of arousing his friend" would be false.[6] Therefore the first statement does not imply the second.

We may contrast, somewhat schematically, the two locutions "He made *p* happen in the endeavour to make *q* happen" and "He made *p* happen for the purpose of making *q*

6 The second statement would be false even if the man *knew* that the chickens were there and that by blowing the horn he would make them fly. In such a case, we could say he made them fly *voluntarily* but we could not say he did anything *for the purpose* of making them fly or that he did anything *with the intention* of making them fly. Compare St. Thomas: "If a man wills some cause from which he knows a particular effect results, it follows that he wills that effect. Although perhaps he does not intend that effect in itself, nevertheless he rather wishes that the effect exist than that the cause not exist." *Commentary on Aristotle's Ethics*, paragraph 512; the passage pertains to Book III, Ch. 5, 1114a.

happen." The second of these two locutions implies the first, but the first does not imply the second. We may say that each of them is teleological with respect to its second propositional component, for each of them implies "He did something for the purpose of making q happen." The second locution, unlike the first, is also teleological with respect to its first component, for, although it may not imply "He did something for the purpose of making q happen," it does imply "He intentionally made q happen."[7] And the second locution, although it does not imply success with respect to the teleology of the second component, does imply success with respect to the teleology of the first component.

I suggest that, to understand the interrelations among the concepts of the theory of action, we take the first of these two locutions as undefined and then exhibit the structure of other, more complex concepts by defining them in terms of it. Let us expand the locution to this:

> At t, he contributes causally to its happening that --- in the endeavour to contribute causally to its happening that ...

where the blanks may be filled by any well-formed sentences or by open sentences. The awkward expression "he contributes causally to its happening that ---" has these advantages over the simpler "he makes it happen that ---": it does not imply that the agent is in any sense a "total cause" of the things he makes happen; and it enables us to apply the locution to situations in which, although it would be accurate to say that the agent contributes causally to making a certain thing happen, it would be inaccurate or misleading to say simply that he "caused" those things or that he "made them happen." We shall interpret "he contributes causally to its happening that ---" in such a way that, like "he makes it happen that ---," it implies that the event or state of affairs

---

7 The reasons for distinguishing "He did something for the purpose of making q happen" and "He intentionally made q happen" is that, in the case of so-called basic actions, the second locution will be true and the first false. We return to this distinction below.

in question does occur. And where no misunderstanding is likely to arise, we may allow ourselves the simpler locution, "He makes it happen that --- in the endeavour to make it happen that ... ," as well as such variations as these: "He makes it happen that --- and does so in the endeavour to make it happen that ..."; and "In the endeavour to make it happen that ... , he makes it happen that ---." The locution may also be varied in other obvious ways – for example, by substituting a description or proper name for the subject-term or for the temporal variable, and by introducing tenses.

It should be emphasized (1) that the expression "he contributes causally to its happening that ---" may have no use in ordinary language, (2) that the simpler expression "he makes it happen that ---" may have a use in ordinary language that is more restricted than the one we allow ourselves here, and (3) that one would hardly be likely to understand our undefined locution if one did not already know what an action is.[8] But from these facts it hardly follows that it would be unsuitable to take this locution as undefined in a logic of intentional action. For the locution *is* clear as it stands and, as I shall try to show, it provides us with the means of developing a vocabulary that is adequate to the theory of action.

IV

We now introduce the following abbreviation of our undefined locution, "At t he contributes causally to its happening that --- in the endeavour to contribute causally to its happening that ...":

M^t---, ...

8 Some of these points are emphasized by Terence Penelhum in "Doing, Desiring, and Making Happen," *Journal of Philosophy*, 20 (1964), 625–627, and by Irving Thalberg, in "Do We Cause our Own Actions?" in *Analysis*, 27 (1967), 196–201. Compare Max Black, "Making Something Happen," in *Determinism and Freedom in the Age of Modern Science*, edited by Sidney Hook (New York: New York University Press, 1958), pp. 15–30.

(A term designating the agent could be introduced into this abbreviation in the form of a subscript, but for simplicity we shall keep such reference implicit.)

We now formulate six assumptions concerning the interpretation of our locution. The first is suggested by the fact that if our agent made the chickens fly in the endeavour to arouse his friend, then there was something such that in the endeavour to make that something happen he made the chickens fly, and also there was something such that he made that something happen in the endeavour to arouse his friend.

AI   Any instance of "M^t---, ..." implies "$(\exists p)(\exists q)(M^t p,q)$."

In other words, wherever our locution is applicable, then there is some state of affairs p and some state of affairs q such that the agent contributes causally to p's obtaining in the endeavour to contribute causally to q's obtaining.[9]

---

9 Hence it would be more accurate to replace the second formula quoted in AI by "$(\exists p)(\exists q)[M^t(p$ obtains), q obtains]"; for the blanks in our undefined locution are to be filled either by sentences or by open sentences. But for simplicity we omit the verb "obtains" in AI and in several of the definitions that appear below. We may note also that the use of state-of-affairs variables does not preclude the use, in the same context, of individual variables. "The dog is such that he believes it to be brown" implies, not only "$(\exists x)$ (he believes x to be brown)," but also "$(\exists p)$ (he believes p to be true)," or alternatively "$(\exists p)$ (he believes p to obtain)," and therefore it may be said to imply "$(\exists x)(\exists p)$ (he believes x to be red and he believes p to be true)." Hence we should also consider such formulae as the following:

A $(\exists x)(\exists y)[M^t(..x..), ..y..]$
B $(\exists y)[M^t(\exists x)(..x..), ..y..]$
C $(\exists x)M^t(..x..), (\exists y)(..y..)$
D $M^t(\exists x)(..x..), (\exists y)(..y..)$

I suggest that: A and B are logically equivalent; C and D are logically equivalent; and A implies C, but not conversely. The second component in each of these formulae expresses an intentional phenomenon ("in the endeavour to") and therefore it is referentially opaque. In other words, the fact that two expressions (say "Jones" and "the thief") happen to designate the same object and the fact that one of them occurs in our second component ("in the endeavour to make it happen that the police find out the name of the thief") are not together sufficient to warrant replacing the one by the other in our second component ("in the endeavour to make it happen that the police find out the name of Jones"). It is sometimes said that it is "illegitimate" to quantify into opaque contexts, as we do in A and B above. But this dictum may

We assume, secondly, that if our locution is true, then its first component is also true:

A2   Any instance of "M^t---, ..." implies the corresponding instance of "---."

If the man of our example made the chickens fly in the endeavour to arouse his friend, then the chickens did fly. It may be, however, that the man was not aroused; hence we do not assume that any instance of "M^t---, ..." implies the corresponding instance of "... ."[10]

We shall assume, third, that our locution is expandable in the following respect. It implies a locution of its own form in which it itself is the first component and in which its own second component is the second component. In other words:

A3   Any instance of "M^t---, ..." implies the corresponding instance of "$M^t(M^t$---, ...), ..."

If our man contributed causally to the flying of the chickens, and did so in the endeavour to arouse his friend, then (i) his making the chickens fly in the endeavour to arouse his friend is something he made happen and, moreover, (ii) it is something he made happen in the endeavour to arouse his friend.

be taken in two somewhat different senses. (1) It may be taken to mean that existential generalization is not generally valid with respect to opaque contexts; "Jones believes that the witch is ferocious" does not imply "($\exists x$) (Jones believes that x is ferocious)," and C and D above do not imply A or B. Or (2) it may be taken to mean that the results of existentially generalizing into such contexts are never true; no sentence of the form "($\exists x$) (Jones believes that x is ferocious)," or of the form of A or B above, is ever true. I suggest that in sense (1) the dictum is obviously true and that in sense (2) it is obviously false. Sometimes it is assumed, unfortunately, that in order to show (2) to be true it is sufficient to show (1) to be true.

10 May the temporal variable be moved from the M-operator to the first propositional component? Let us recall that, strictly, the proper reading of "M" is, not "He makes it happen that," but "He contributes causally to its happening that." Since a man may make a causal contribution now to some future event, we should not say that "M^t---, ..." implies "---at t." Hence we may not say, generally, that the temporal variable may be moved from the M-operator to the first propositional component.

This third assumption may be suggested by an observation Suarez makes in this context: "If we understand the term 'effect' so that it includes not only the thing produced, but also everything that flows from the power of the agent, then we may say that the action itself is in a certain sense the effect of the agent."[11]

Our fourth assumption concerns what we might call "the transitivity of non-occurrent causation." I have said that the present paper presupposes a distinction between "occurrent causation" and "non-occurrent causation" – between saying that a state of affairs or set of states of affairs causes a certain state of affairs to obtain, and saying that a person causes a certain state of affairs to obtain. Occurrent causation is transitive, at least in the following respect: if the occurrence of one state of affairs contributes causally to the occurrence of a second state of affairs, and if the occurrence of a second state of affairs, in turn, contributes causally to that of a third, then the occurrence of the first may be said to contribute causally to the occurrence of the third. The causal contribution made by a person may be viewed analogously.

Let us say, then, that if an agent contributes causally to the occurrence of a given state of affairs and if the occurrence of this state of affairs contributes causally to the occurrence of another state of affairs, then the agent contributes causally to the occurrence of that other state of affairs. Using "pCq" as an abbreviation for "p's obtaining contributes causally to q's obtaining," or "the occurrence of p contributes causally to the occurrence of q," we may put our fourth assumption as follows:

A4 $(p)(q)(r)\{[(M^tp,q) \ \& \ (pCr)] \supset (M^tr,q)\}$

Here it is essential that we read "M^tp" as "He contributed

11 F. Suarez, *Disputationes Metaphysicae*, Disp. XVIII, Sec. 10, Para. 6. Compare Robert Binkley, "A Theory of Practical Reason," *Philosophical Review*, 74 (1965), 423–448; Binkley assumes that "He brings it about that p" ("Cp") implies "He brings it about that he brings it about that p" ("CCp").

causally at *t* to making *p* happen," and not simply as "At *t* he made *p* happen." Suppose that by driving slowly a man contributes causally to a second man being late for dinner (the second man, who was in the car behind, missed the evening ferry), and suppose the second man's being late for dinner contributed causally to the annoyance of his wife. It would be at least misleading to say, in such a situation, that the first man made it happen that the wife of the second man was annoyed, or that he was morally responsible for her annoyance (it wasn't *his* fault), or that *he* annoyed her (it was her husband and not he who was the intentional object of her annoyance). But he did contribute causally to her being annoyed, for, we may suppose, if he had not driven as he did she would not have been annoyed. And let us note the constancy of the temporal variable in this formula. If the driving took place at five and the annoyance at seven, then it was at five, and not at seven, that the driver contributed causally to the lady's annoyance.[12]

There is still a problem to be solved with respect to the interpretation of our undefined locution. Of the things a man makes happen at a given time, is it possible for (i) some to be such that he makes them happen in one endeavour, (ii) some to be such that he makes them happen in another endeavour, and (iii) some of those he makes happen in the one endeavour *not* to be among those he makes happen in the other endeavour? Could it be, for example, that while our agent is making one thing happen in the endeavour to arouse his friend, he is making another thing happen in the endeavour to keep his car on the road, and that the thing he is making

---

12 Compare the problems involved in answering "When did the assassin murder the victim?" if it is known that he put the fatal dose in the glass at five, that the victim drank the potion at six, and that the victim died at seven. But there is no occasion to ask, with respect to our example above, "When did the driver annoy the lady?" For even if the driver had brought about the whole affair intentionally, thereby successfully bringing it about that she was annoyed (see D6 below), it would not be accurate to say that he *annoyed* the lady. See the discussion of such questions in H. L. A. Hart and A. M. Honoré, *Causation in the Law* (Oxford: The Clarendon Press, 1962), Ch. 3.

happen in the endeavour to arouse his friend is not one of the things he is making happen in the endeavour to keep his car on the road? In such a case, the following would be true:

$$(M^t p,q) \;\&\; (M^t r,s) \;\&\; \sim(M^t r,q)$$

If this situation is possible, then we must face the problem of distinguishing the "p" and the "r" in our formula; we must find some reason for saying that the one but not the other is something he made happen in the endeavour to make q happen.

But is the situation possible? Can a man thus make two separate endeavours at one and the same time? He can, of course, make separate endeavours at different times. The formula above could be true if the time referred to in the first conjunct were different from that referred to in the second and third. And a man can, at a given time, endeavour to make more than one thing happen at that time. That is to say, a conjunctive state of affairs may be the object of his endeavour, as suggested by the formula:

$$M^t p, (r \;\&\; s)$$

But I suggest that a man cannot make two separate endeavours at one and the same time. Thus if there is a certain moment at which our agent makes something happen in the endeavour to arouse his friend, and if at *precisely that same moment* he is making something happen to keep his car on the road, then it will not be the case that there is something he is making happen in one endeavour which he is not making in the other endeavour. The object of his endeavour is that conjunctive state of affairs which is his friend being aroused and his car staying on the road; whatever he may be said to be making happen on behalf of the one conjunct he is also making happen on behalf of the other.

There is an impressive tradition behind this way of looking at the matter. Thus St. Thomas says: "One power cannot have several acts at the same time, except in so far as it might occur that one act is comprised in another; just as neither can a body have several shapes, except in so far as one shape enters into another, as a three-sided in a four-sided figure."[13] Let us say, in our terminology, that if a man makes what are clearly two distinct endeavours, then the time at which he makes the one will be different from the time at which he makes the other.

We may express the desired axioms by using two temporal variables and saying that, if the agent makes something p happen in the endeavour to make something q happen, and if he makes something r happen in the endeavour to make something s happen but *not* in the endeavour to make q happen, then the time at which he makes p happen is different from the time at which he makes r happen.

A5 $\quad (p)(q)(r)(s)\{[(M^t p, q) \,\&\, (M^{t'} r, s) \,\&\, \sim(M^{t'} r, q)] \supset \sim(t = t')\}$

This axiom will make clear that the sense of intentional action with which we are here concerned is more strict than what may be suggested by the ordinary use of the verb "doing." For, although there are obvious senses in which a man may be said to do many different things at one time, our axiom tells that, so far as his exercise of "non-occurrent causation" is concerned, any two such acts will be at different times. Thus the axiom could be expressed by saying "A man can make only one endeavour at a time." But it may *not* be expressed by saying "A man can endeavour to bring about only one thing at a time."

Still another principle should be added to our list of axioms: if a man makes a conjunction of things happen in a certain endeavour, then he may be said to make each of those things happen in that endeavour; and conversely.

A6 $\quad (p)(q)(r)\{[(M^t p, q) \,\&\, (M^t r, q)] \equiv M^t (p \,\&\, r), q\}$

13 *Summa Theologica*, I–II, q. 54, art. 1, ad. 3. Compare also I, q. 58, art. 7, ad. 2; as well as Duns Scotus, *Ordinatio*, I, d. 17, n. 43 (Vatican Edition, Vol. V, p. 156) and *Opus Oxoniense*, III, d. 26, n. 21 (Vives edition, Vol. XV, p. 344). I am indebted to the Reverend Allan B. Wolter for these references.

But let us note that, in affirming A6, we are *not* affirming the following:

$$(p)(q)(r)\{[M^tp,(q \ \& \ r)] \supset M^tp,r\}$$

I may do something in the endeavour to contribute causally to the truth of that conjunction which is my being at the meeting and your being at the meeting and yet not do anything in the endeavour to contribute causally to your being at the meeting.

Let us note that our axioms A2, A3, and A6, respectively, are analogues of the following familiar modal principles:

$$Np \supset p$$
$$Np \supset NNp$$
$$(Np \ \& \ Nr) \equiv N(p \ \& \ r)$$

For, making use of AI and abbreviating, we see that our principles become:

$$M^tp,q \supset p$$
$$M^tp,q \supset M^t(M^tp,q),q$$
$$[(M^tp,q) \ \& \ (M^tr,q)] \equiv M^t(p \ \& \ r),q$$

A different notation would bring out the analogy more clearly.[14] Thus instead of "He makes *p* happen in the endeavour to make *q* happen" (or its more accurate expanded version), we might have said "Undertaking to make *q* happen, he makes *p* happen"; then, instead of "M^tp,q" we could have written "U^tq,p"; and then we could have transformed "U^tq,p" to "Q^tp," letting capitalization do the work of "*U*." And now removing the temporal variable (a temporary device just to make the analogy more striking), we now see clearly the resemblance between our three principles and the three modal principles. For our principles become:

$$Qp \supset p$$
$$Qp \supset QQp$$
$$(Qp \ \& \ Qr) \equiv Q(p \ \& \ r)$$

---

14 A notation similar to the alternative proposed here was first suggested to me by Hector-Neri Castañeda.

V

Now we may set forth a series of definitions which, I believe, will explicate some of the fundamental concepts that are involved in the theory of action.

We begin with a concept for which we may use either the verb "to undertake" or the verb "to endeavour." It is a concept that philosophers sometimes express by means of the verb "to try."[15] But "to try" is misleading inasmuch as it connotes exerting an effort, whereas the concept with which we are concerned does not. Our full expression will be "He undertakes at *t* to contribute causally to its happening that ..." or, more briefly, "He undertakes at *t* to make it happen that ..."; we may also use "endeavours" in place of "undertakes." We abbreviate this expression as "$U^t(...)$" and define it as follows:

DI $U^t(...) = \mathrm{Df}\ (\exists p)(M^t p, ...)$

In other words, he undertakes at *t* to make it happen that ..., provided only there is some state of affairs *p* such that at *t* he makes it happen that *p* obtains and he does so in the endeavour to make it happen that ....

Now we may introduce two senses of "making happen" – two senses of "contributing causally to making a certain thing happen." Let us introduce "$A^t(---)$" as an abbreviation for "At *t* he makes it happen that ---," or, more accurately, an abbreviation for "At *t* he contributes causally to its happening that ---."[16] The expression may now be defined as follows:

15 I think it is clear that G. E. Moore was using "try" to express this concept in the following: "That the bird's *body* moves away, owing to its wings moving in a certain way, is not *all* we mean by saying *it flies* away: as Wittgenstein says, if *I raise* my arm, something else happens *beside* that *my* arm is raised: that *I raise* it is a *Handlung*, and this is what we mean by saying that the raising is due to my *will*, though I neither *choose* nor *decide*. When I *choose* or *decide*, all that happens may be that I *try* to raise it." G. E. Moore, *Commonplace Book 1919–1953*, edited by C. Lewy (London: George Allen & Unwin, 1962), p. 410.

16 We have noted that "He makes it happen that ---" has this advantage

D2 $A^t(\text{---}) = \text{Df} (\exists p)(M^t\text{---}, p)$

In other words, at *t* he makes it happen that ---, provided only there is some state of affairs *p* such that at *t* he makes it happen that --- in the endeavour to make it happen that *p* obtains. The concept we have defined is not the concept of *making something happen intentionally* (for our man made the chickens fly but did not do so intentionally); yet it does pertain to an *intentional act* in that it refers to something the agent made happen in the *endeavour* to make something happen. Thus it will not apply to those things which, as we may sometimes say, the agent "does" while he is asleep, or unconscious, or otherwise not endeavouring to do anything at all. Thus if the agent twitches uncontrollably and thereby knocks over the table, we may say that knocking over the table is something that he "did," but it will not pertain to an intentional act in the sense of the present expression, for it will not imply that there is something such that our agent knocked over the table in the endeavour to bring about that something.

We may now define a very broad sense of the expression "intentional act." We will express this by the locution "At *t* he intentionally contributes causally to its happening that ---," which may be abbreviated as "$IA^t(\text{---})$" and defined as follows:

D3 $IA^t(\text{---}) = \text{Df } Mt\text{---}, \text{---}$

This is a very broad sense of "intentional action" for it will apply to what we may call "inadvertent successes." Suppose the assassin takes aim with the intention of killing his victim; in so doing, he inadvertently knocks over the paint cans and

over the longer locution, "He contributes causally to making it happen that ---": the shorter locution makes it clear that the event referred to by the expression in the place of the blank *does* occur; but the longer locution might suggest, to some, that that event does not occur. With A2 we make explicit our stipulation concerning the interpretation of "He contributes causally to making it happen that ---": it implies the corresponding instance of "---."

the falling of the paint cans has the effect of killing the victim. In such a case, our broad definition of "intentional action" would be satisfied since, in the endeavour to bring it about that the victim died, our agent did in fact bring it about that the victim died. But we are not likely to want to say, in such a case, that the death was brought about intentionally.[17] We shall define a less broad sense of intentional action in D6 below.

Some of the consequences of our definitions and axioms may be summarized in this way: Making a certain state of affairs p happen implies that p does happen, but it does not imply undertaking to make p happen. Undertaking to make p happen does not imply that p does happen and therefore it does not imply making p happen. But intentionally making p happen implies both undertaking to make p happen and also making p happen. Making p happen implies making happen making p happen. And undertaking to make p happen implies making something or other q happen in the endeavour to make p happen; but it does not imply making anything happen in the endeavour to make that something or other q happen. Again, undertaking to make p happen implies *making happen undertaking to make p happen*, but it does not imply *undertaking to undertake* to make p happen.

VI

Now we may return to the concept of *purpose*. We have said that "He makes the chickens fly *in the endeavour* to arouse his friend" does not imply "He makes the chickens fly *for the*

17 What if the bullet had missed its mark, but the firing of the shot brought about the falling of the staging and the falling of the staging, in turn, brought about the death of the victim? The definition of a completely successful intentional action which we shall introduce below D6 will enable us to say that this was not a completely successful intentional action and thus provide us with a sense, if we want one, in which we may say that, even here, the death was not brought about intentionally.

purpose of arousing his friend," for the second expression, we said, is teleological with respect to both propositional components, whereas the first is teleological only with respect to the second. Using the terminology just introduced, we may say that the second expression, unlike the first, implies not only that the agent undertook to arouse his friend but also that he undertook to make the chickens fly. Part of his endeavour was to make the chickens fly; another part of it was to contribute causally to the arousal of his friend by undertaking to make the chickens fly. (Why not say, more simply: "another part of it was to contribute causally to the arousal of his friend by making the chickens fly"? We will consider this question below.) We must, therefore, import the concept of causation into our definition of purpose, or purposive action.

Reading "*C*" as "contributes causally to," let us introduce the following notation: "{---}*C*{...}." The braces indicate that the blanks are to be filled by the gerundive versions of well-formed sentences. Thus any instance of "--- & {---}*C* {...}" will have a well-formed sentence in the place of the first blank and its gerundive version in the place of the second.

Abbreviating "At t he contributes causally to making it happen that --- *for the purpose of* contributing causally to making it happen that ..." by "$P^t(M^t$---, ...)," let us consider the following definition:

D4 $P^t(M^t$---, ...) = Df M^t---, [--- & {U^t---}C{...}]

To say that our man made the chickens fly for the purpose of arousing his friend, if this definition is adequate, would be to say that the man made the chickens fly and that he did so in the endeavour to bring about two things – first, that the chickens would fly, and, secondly, that that activity of his by means of which he brings this about would also be one that brings about the arousal of his friend. Since he acted in the endeavour to bring about these two things, we may also say that he *undertook* to bring about these two things.

This definition of purposive activity may seem needlessly complex. Let us consider, therefore, certain possible ways of simplifying it.

The following definition would be much simpler:

$$P^t(M^t\text{---}, ...) = \text{Df } M^t(U^t\text{---}), ...$$

Simplifying the English reading, we could say that "He made p happen for the purpose of making q happen" is here defined as "He made it happen that he undertook to make p happen and he did so in the endeavour to make q happen." When the definiendum is true, then the proposed definiens will also be true. But it may be, however, that when the definiendum is false, the proposed definiens will be true – when, instead of making p happen for the purpose of making q happen, our agent is making q happen for the purpose of making p happen.

Why not delete the first conjunct of the second part of our original definiens? In this case, we would have:

$$P^t(M^t\text{---}, ...) = \text{Df } M^t\text{---}, [\{U^t\text{---}\}C\{...\}]$$

Wasn't the first conjunct, namely "---," redundant? If the man undertook to make it happen that his endeavours to make the chickens fly would bring about the arousal of his friend, then *didn't* he endeavour to make the chickens fly? It would seem to be logically possible for a man to undertake this without making the corresponding endeavour. It is obvious, of course, that at one time a man may deceive himself into thinking that he has made certain endeavours at another time (he may congratulate himself on the endeavours he has made to resist temptation). Conceivably an irrational man may endeavour to bring it about that certain of his present endeavours cause something – even though he isn't making the endeavours in question. If this strange situation is logically possible, then we should retain the first conjunct.[18]

18 Should we add, then, a *third* conjunct, namely "...," to the second part of our definiens, thus saying that the man of our example undertook to bring it about that his friend was aroused? We could add this, but I suggest it follows from what we already have and therefore that it

C

But why the "*U*" in the second conjunct? Why say that what he undertook was that his endeavour to make the chickens fly would bring about the arousal of the friend? Why not say, more simply, that he undertook to bring it about that the flying of the chickens would cause the arousal of the friend? In such a case our definition would read:

$$P^t(M^t\text{---}, \ldots) = \text{Df } M^t\text{---}, [\text{---} \ \& \ \{\text{---}\}C\{\ldots\}]$$

To see the disadvantage of this simpler definition, we should consider a somewhat different type of case. Consider a man who dislodges a stone at the top of the hill and aims it toward a certain cabin below. He endeavours to bring it about that the stone will hit the cabin, but his purpose in so doing is to bring it about that the stone traverses a certain intermediate place between himself and the cabin. (The only way he can assure himself that the stone *will* traverse this intermediate place is by assuring himself that the stone will hit the cabin.) We may say, of this situation, that the agent destroyed the cabin in order that the stone would traverse a certain area. Or, in our terminology, he made it happen that the cabin was destroyed for the purpose of making it happen that the stone traversed a certain area. But the simpler definition above does not capture this situation. The simpler definition would require us to say that he undertook to make it happen that the cabin was destroyed and that the destruction of the cabin would cause the stone to traverse the area in question. But the destruction of the cabin, as he knew, would be subsequent to the traversal of the area and therefore, being rational, he was not undertaking to make the destruction of the cabin cause the traversal of the area. What he was undertaking to do was, rather, to bring about that his endeavour to destroy the cabin would bring about the traversal of the area.[19] This is why we need the more complex definition.

would be redundant. For if he endeavoured to bring it about that his endeavours would bring it about that his friend was aroused, then, surely, he endeavoured to bring it about that his friend was aroused.

19 This situation may recall the scholastic distinction between the *finis*

Other examples of this need are provided by the following: the man who brings it about that a tree will grow next year for the purpose of collecting his pay next week; and the man who makes his arm go up for the purposes of activating those causes in his brain that will bring it about that his arm goes up.

Thus we can distinguish "Making the chickens fly and doing so for the purpose of arousing one's friend" from our primitive, "Making the chickens fly and doing so in the endeavour to arouse one's friend." The first of these expressions – the one we have just defined – may be said to be teleological with respect *both* to the first component and to the second component; but the second expression – our primitive – is teleological only with respect to the second component. And now we may contrast these two expressions with a third: "Undertaking to make the chickens fly and doing so for the purpose of arousing one's friend." This third expression, like the first and unlike the second, is teleological with respect to the first and second components. But unlike the first and the second, it does not imply the truth of the first component: it does not imply that the agent was successful in undertaking to make the chickens fly.

These three locutions may thus be said to represent three levels of intentionality: the first expression is teleological with respect to the second component but does not imply success with respect to the second component; the *third* expression is teleological with respect to both components and does not imply success with respect to either component; and the second expression is teleological with respect to both components and implies success with respect to the first component but not with respect to the second component.

operantis, the aim of the operator or agent, and the *finis operationis*, the aim of his operation or activity. Compare the discussion of means-end reasoning in Binkley, "A Theory of Practical Reason," p. 443: "... means-end reasoning requires not merely a judgment about the interconnections of things, but also a kind of self-conscious judgment of one's own effectiveness as an agent causing things to happen."

We may express this third locution somewhat more accurately as "At t he undertakes to contribute causally to its happening that --- and does so for the purpose of making it happen that ...." We may abbreviate it as "$P^t(U^t$---, ...)" and define it as follows:

D5 $P^t(U^t$---, ...$) = \text{Df}(\exists p)\{M^t p,[$--- & $\{U^t$---$\}C\{...\}]\}$

If the man undertook to make the chickens fly and did so for the purpose of arousing his friend, then, according to this definition, there is something or other he made happen in the endeavour, first, to make the chickens fly and, second, to make this endeavour cause the arousal of his friend.

With the concept that has been defined in D5, that of undertaking something p for the purpose of bringing about something q, we are able to define three further concepts that are essential to the theory of intentional action. These are: the concept of undertaking something "for its own sake"; the concept of a completely successful intentional action; and the concept of a "basic action."

VII

It seems clear that any account of purposive activity ought to be adequate to the following distinctions. Thus (1) there are certain things we bring about merely in order to bring about certain other things; we submit to an unpleasant remedy, for example, for the sake of a subsequent cure. (2) There are certain things we bring about "for their own sakes," or "for themselves alone"; certain pleasurable activities are obvious examples. And it would seem that (3) on occasion there are certain things we undertake *both* in order to bring about still other things *and also* as "ends in themselves" or "for their own sakes." Deprecating amusement as an end in itself, Aristotle quotes Anacharsis who said that it is proper "to amuse oneself in order that one may exert oneself."[20]

20 *Ethics*, Book X, Ch. 6, 1176b.

Suppose a man could choose between two ways of bringing it about that he could exert himself later: one of them a regimen indifferent in itself and the other a matter of amusing himself, and the two methods being equally harmless. In such a case, a reasonable man would be likely to choose the second method: he would amuse himself for the sake of amusing himself and also for the sake of exerting himself later. Again, of two medicines that are equally effective, a reasonable man would choose the one that is pleasant rather than the one that is not – in which case, he would take the pleasant medicine partly for the sake of just taking the medicine and partly for the sake of the subsequent cure.[21]

Were it not for the third category, those things we bring about both for their own sakes and also for the sake of certain other things as well, we could formulate a relatively simple definition of bringing about something for its own sake. We could say merely that those things we undertake to bring about for the sake of other things are those things p which we undertake to bring about for the purpose of bringing about some other thing q; and then we could say that those things we undertake to bring about for their own sakes are those things p which we undertake to bring about, but which we do not undertake to bring about for the purpose of bringing about some other thing q. But such a definition would not allow us to say that a man takes a pleasant medicine both for the sake of taking it and also for the sake of the subsequent cure.

I suggest we say this: the man who takes the medicine both as an end in itself and also for the purpose of the subsequent cure undertakes a conjunctive state of affairs, that he take the medicine and that he be cured, and he does so for the purpose, in part, of taking the medicine; and the man

21 Compare St. Thomas, *Commentary of Aristotle's Ethics*, Para. 109: "We find also an object is indeed desirable on account of what it is, but besides, it is desired for something else, like sweet-tasting medicine."

who takes the indifferent medicine merely for the purpose of the subsequent cure and not as an end in itself undertakes a similar conjunctive state of affairs, that he take the medicine and that he be cured; but the second man, unlike the first man, does *not* undertake this conjunctive state of affairs for the purpose, even in part, of taking the medicine. More exactly, if a man is undertaking a certain thing p for its own sake, or as an end in itself, then the following will be true: if there is anything q that does not entail p and is such that he undertakes p for the sake of q, then he is undertaking the conjunction of p and q for the sake, in part, of p; and if he is undertaking p, but as a means only and not as an end in itself, then he will be undertaking such a conjunction, p and q, but not for the sake of p.

Reading the arrow "→" as "entails," and abbreviating "At t he undertakes as an *end in itself* to bring about that ---" by "$U^tE(---)$", let us add the following definition:

D6 $U^tE(---) = \text{Df } (q)\{[\sim(q \rightarrow ---) \,\&\, P^t(U^t---,q)] \supset P^t[U^t(--- \,\&\, q),---]\}$

Given this concept, it will be obvious how to draw the distinctions referred to above.

VIII

Next we refine upon the concept of making something happen intentionally that was introduced in D3. A man could be said to make something happen intentionally, in that very broad sense, provided only he makes a certain thing happen in the endeavour to make that thing happen. But this sense is too broad, we said, for it allows the possibility of "inadvertent success." But now, given the concept that was introduced in D5, we may define a *completely successful* intentional action. We express this concept by the locution, "At t he contributes causally to its happening that --- and is completely successful with respect to the means he adopts." We abbreviate the locution as "$S^tIA(\text{---})$" and define it as follows:

D7 $S^tIA(\text{---})$ = Df $IA^t(\text{---})$ & $(p)[P^t(U^tp,\text{---}) \supset Ap]$

If a man was *completely* successful in the endeavours he made at a certain time to bring about a certain state of affairs, then *everything* he undertook at that time to bring about that state of affairs is something he successfully brought about. Let us recall once again the assassin who achieved an inadvertent success: he shot at the victim and accomplished his goal, not because the bullet hit the mark, as he intended, but because the firing of the gun caused the paint cans to fall on the victim's head and kill him. This act was not a complete success by our present definition, for in the endeavour to bring about the death of his victim, there was something the agent undertook to bring about – the bullet hitting the mark – which was not successful. Therefore we may avoid saying, if we choose, that the assassin brought about the death intentionally.

But is the definition too rigid? Suppose that, as a good marksman, the assassin did succeed in shooting the victim, but that he was also a man of caution and at the same time acted upon an alternative method. And what if the alternative method failed? (As he fired at the victim, he stepped on a lever to activate the trap door, but the lever didn't work.) In such a case, we cannot say, as our definition would have it, that *everything* he undertook for the purpose of bringing about the victim's death was successful. Yet, wasn't he completely successful in what he endeavoured to do with the gun? This is true, but it is no indication that our definition is too rigid. For the definition to be adequate to the successful phase of our assassin's activity, we have only to fill the blank, not by "the victim dies," but by "the victim dies as a result of gunshot."

IX

And now we may define "basic actions" – those things we do without having to do other things to get them done.[22] For most of us, raising our arms and blinking our eyes are actions that are thus basic; unlike wiggling our ears, they are such that we do not have to do *other* things for the purpose of getting them done. Let us introduce the expression, "At *t* he makes it happen that --- and his doing so is a *basic act* at *t*," and abbreviate it as "$B^t(---)$." Our definition of basic action will be:

D8 $B^t(---) = \text{Df } IA^t(---) \ \& \sim(\exists p)[P^t(U^t p,---)]$

In other words, he performs so-and-so as a basic act at *t* provided that he brought about so-and-so intentionally at *t* and provided further that there was nothing he undertook at *t* for the purpose of bringing so-and-so about.

Given this definition of basic action, we need not say, as Danto does, that a man's basic actions are actions "which he cannot be said to have caused to happen." We may say, if we choose, that a man may undertake a basic act on a certain occasion and fail. Presumably this would happen, if unknown to himself, the man had lost some member of what Danto calls his "repertoire" of basic actions and then discovers the loss. On such an occasion, the following would be true:

$$U^t(---) \ \& \sim(\exists p[P^t(U^t p,---)] \ \& \sim A^t(---)$$

We may also say that a man's basic acts are a subclass of those acts with respect to which he is completely successful. For, although a basic act, like every other intentional act, is something that the agent undertakes, it is not something which is such that he undertakes some *other* thing for the purpose of bringing it about. The definiens of D6, therefore, is satisfied;

22 This term was introduced by Arthur Danto in "What We Can Do,"
Journal of Philosophy, 60 (1963), 435–445, reprinted in Alan R. White,
The Philosophy of Action (London: Oxford University Press, 1968).
Compare St. Augustine, *The City of God*, Book XIV, Ch. 24.

since he doesn't undertake anything for the purpose of bringing about the basic act, it may be said that everything he undertakes for the purpose of bringing about the basic act is something that he does bring about.

X

Finally, we will attempt to confirm what has been said by applying it to certain philosophical puzzles.[23]

1 "A responsible act is an act such that, at the time at which the agent undertook to perform it, he had it within his power to perform the act and also within his power not to perform the act. But physiology seems to tell us that what the agent thus accomplishes is caused by certain physiological events. (The man raises his arm; certain cerebral and muscular events cause the arm to go up.) How, then, can the act be said to be something that was then in his power not to perform?"

The agent was such that, in the endeavour to make it happen that his arm go up, he made it happen (i) that the various physiological states, including the cerebral and muscular events, occurred, and also (ii) that his arm went up. Since he made (i) occur, and since (i) contributed causally to the occurrence of (ii), he may also be said to have contributed causally to the occurrence of (ii); see A4.

2 "If a man has learned what the muscle motions are that cause his arm to go up, and if, in the course of a physical examination, he wishes to move those muscles, then he can do so by raising his arm. Physiology tells us, however, that the muscle motions cause the arm to go up. And causation is asymmetrical: if a particular event p is the cause of a particular event q, then q cannot be the cause of p. The cause, moreover, cannot occur after the effect. How, then, can he move his muscles by raising the arm?"

23 Some but not all of these puzzles were presented in the writings cited in footnote 1.

The man who moves his muscles by raising his arm makes it happen that his arm goes up for the purpose of making it happen that his muscles move. This means that he undertakes to make it happen that his *endeavour* to make the arm go up will make it happen that the muscles move; see D4. It does not mean that he undertook to make it happen that his arm going up would make it happen that the muscles move. We may recall the man who undertook to bring it about that the cabin would be destroyed (the *finis operationis*) for the purpose of bringing about the prior traversal of the cliff (the *finis operans*).

3 "(a) A man cannot perform an intentional act unless there is something that he endeavours or undertakes to perform; and whenever he performs an act successfully, then he performs what it was that he endeavoured to perform. (b) Whenever a man performs an intentional act, then he brings it about that he does perform that act, and whenever he endeavours or undertakes to perform an act, then he brings it about that he endeavours or undertakes to perform that act; hence a man's undertaking or endeavours may be counted among his acts and therefore among his intentional acts. (c) But these theses imply the absurd conclusion that if a man undertakes or endeavours to do a certain thing, then he endeavours to endeavour to do that thing, or he undertakes to undertake to do that thing.[24] How can this be?"

The answer is simply that the absurd conclusion does *not* follow from the premisses. As we have noted: making something p happen implies undertaking to make something q happen; making p happen also implies making happen making p happen; undertaking to make something q happen implies making something p happen and it also implies making happen undertaking to make q happen; but it does not imply undertaking to undertake to make q happen.

4 "Oedipus' father was identical with Laius, the offensive

24 Compare Hobbes: "I acknowledge this liberty, that I can do if I will: but to say, I can will if I will, I take to be an absurd speech."

traveller. Oedipus intended to kill the offensive traveller, but he certainly did not intend to kill his own father. Yet the killing of the offensive traveller *was* the killing of Oedipus' father. Hence we must say of this event that it *was* intentional and also that it was *not* intentional. How can this be?"

That state of affairs which was the killing of the offensive traveller was *not* the same as that state of affairs which was the killing of Oedipus' father; the former, for example, implies that someone was an offensive traveller but the latter does not, and the latter implies that Oedipus had a father but the former does not. Yet there was a sense in which we may say that Oedipus' act was both intentional and non-intentional. But in this sense "intentional" and "non-intentional" are not contraries, since "Oedipus' act was both intentional and non-intentional" is elliptical for "Oedipus' act was intentional with respect to one thing and non-intentional with respect to another thing." What he did was intentional with respect to the killing of the unfriendly traveller and non-intentional with respect to the killing of his father – which is to say only that he undertook the one thing but not the other.[25]

5 "If there are any states of affairs that the man himself causes to happen then there must be certain states of affairs q which are such that he causes q to happen without *first* causing still *other* states of affairs p such that p causes q to happen. If there are such 'basic actions,' then raising the arm must be among them, since (if our agent is like most of the rest of us) there is nothing else he needs to *do* in order to raise his arm. But if the motion of his arm is caused by physiological events, then there are no 'basic actions.' And therefore

25 Since Oedipus actually laid hands upon the unfriendly traveller, we may say that there was an x, namely, the unfriendly traveller, which was such that Oedipus undertook to bring about the death of x. And since the unfriendly traveller was Oedipus' father, we may also say that Oedipus' father was such that Oedipus undertook to bring about his death. But the latter statement does not imply that Oedipus endeavoured to bring about the death of his father; see footnote 9 above.

there is nothing that the agent himself causes to happen."

The third premiss is false. It is not the case that if the motion of his arm is caused by physiological events, then there are no basic actions. "At t he makes q happen and his so doing is a basic act" implies "There is no p such that at t he makes p happen for the purpose of making q happen." But it does not imply "There is no p such that at t he makes p happen and p causes q to happen"; see D8.

6 " ' ... if there are any actions at all, there must be two distinct *kinds* of actions: those performed by an individual M, which he may be said to have *caused* to happen; and those actions, also performed by M, which he cannot be said to have caused to happen. The latter I shall designate as basic actions.' Occasionally people discover that they have lost the ability to perform basic acts; a man discovers, for example, that one of his limbs has become paralysed. How *can* a man discover such a thing unless he does what he usually does for the purpose of performing the act in question and then finds that his attempt is a failure? But if there is something a man usually does for the purpose of performing the supposed 'basic act,' then the act in question is not a basic act. How can this be?"[26]

When a man discovers such a thing, he has not *done* what he usually does for the purpose of performing the basic act in question; that is to say, he has not performed any intentional act for the purpose of performing the basic act. But he did undertake to perform the basic act and failed. There were certain things (some of them entirely unknown to him) that he made happen in the endeavour to make it happen that he move his limb, and although he made these things happen he didn't make it happen that he moved his limb.

7 "Let us not forget this: when 'I raise my arm,' my arm goes up. And the problem arises: what is left over if I subtract

26 The quotation at the beginning is from Danto, "Basic Actions," *American Philosophical Quarterly*, 2 (1965), 141–142. Concerning this type of puzzle, compare G. N. A. Vesey, "Do I Ever Directly Raise My Arm?" *Philosophy*, 42 (1967), 148–149.

the fact that my arm goes up from the fact that I raise my arm?"[27]

What is left over is the fact that I undertook to make my arm go up – the fact that there was something I made happen in the endeavour to make it happen that my arm go up.

27 Ludwig Wittgenstein, *Philosophical Investigations* (Oxford: Blackwell, 1953), p. 161e.

Comments

BY BRUCE AUNE

Professor Chisholm has offered us a very interesting but extremely intricate paper. Although I disagree with some of the basic assumptions on which his system appears to be based – particularly those concerning states of affairs and quantification – I shall direct my remarks chiefly to the axioms and definitions he has carefully formulated.

But first a general point. Chisholm tells us[1] that a more appropriate title for his paper would be "Prolegomena to the Logic of Intentional Action." I agree entirely with this remark. A fully developed logic of intentional action must have a kind of completeness; it must exhibit the basic relations between the entire family of key concepts specifically concerned with intentional action, including *deliberation, choice, decision,* and (I believe) even *volition.* In doing this it must offer some clarification of the logic of practical reasoning, which for philosophers such as Kant is fundamental to the whole subject of intentional action. Since Chisholm's paper (at least as I understand it) makes no pretense of covering the latter topic, it provides only a fragment of a complete logic of intentional action. To say this is not to

1 This remark by Chisholm was included in the original version of his paper read at the conference.

imply, of course, that such a fragment is trivial, uninteresting, or easy to develop.

In discussing his primitive predicate "M'---, ..." Chisholm remarks that it has no exact counterpart in ordinary language. He believes, nevertheless, that his axioms and informal explanations render it "clear as it stands." After pondering his paper for several days, I have concluded that this belief is a bit optimistic. His primitive strikes me as unclear in several crucial respects, and I shall try to illustrate this in the comments that follow.

The interpretation of "M'---, ..." involves the notion of causal contribution. As Chisholm uses this notion, *both* persons and events may be said to contribute causally to the obtaining of states of affairs. Two questions arise from this usage. First, are we to understand that persons and events may contribute causally to something in the *same* sense of the word? This seems very unlikely in view of what Chisholm has said in other papers, but a difference in kinds of causal contribution is not apparent in his present remarks about the transitivity of causal contribution. Second, if a person does contribute causally to some event, are we, or are we not, to conclude that the person actually *initiates* a causal sequence rather than possibly serving as a mere element in such a sequence?

This last question is of crucial importance to what Chisholm eventually says in answer to a familiar puzzle regarding free will. The puzzle is how, if a man's action is caused by certain physiological changes, he could ever have the power either to perform or not to perform that action. Chisholm's answer is that the man himself may have caused the physiological changes in his endeavour to perform the action. This answer is not really satisfactory. If physiology tells us that a man's actions are caused by physiological changes, it equally tells us that these physiological changes are caused by further physiological changes. The basic puzzle therefore remains: Is the agent's causal contribution to certain physiological events really compatible with the causal contribution of further physiological events? And if it is, how is this possible? Until we can answer these questions, we shall not fully understand Chisholm's use of the predicate "M^t---, ..."

I now want to consider two cases that bear upon the question: "Of all the states of affairs to which an agent contributes causally at a time t, how do we identify or delimit those that he makes happen *in his endeavour* to contribute causally to some state of affairs?" I offer first *the case of the frightened burglar*.

At t I make up my mind to frighten a burglar outside my house, and in my endeavour to do so I bring about certain physiological changes in my brain but no observable changes in my posture or position. As it happens, the burglar sees me through the window and is frightened away. Though I am too preoccupied or too absent-minded to realize it at the time, I am still wearing my wolf-man costume, which gives me an extremely frightening appearance. (I have just returned from a party.) The physiological events I have made happen in my brain contribute causally to my total state at t, and my total state in turn contributes causally to frightening the burglar. By Chisholm's axiom A4 and the transitivity of causal contribution we may infer that $M^t(F,F)$, where "F" means "I frighten the burglar." Assuming that I take no other steps to frighten him at t, we may use definition D7 to infer that $S^t IA(F,F)$, which means that I have performed a completely successful intentional act. This seems very odd considering that I have no idea that I have actually frightened anyone, burglar or not.

My next case involves the endeavour to become rich. At time t I refrain from suicide and bank my weekly salary in the endeavour to become rich. At t', later than t, I inherit a large sum of money which, together with my meagre savings, makes me rich. Had I committed suicide at t, I would not have inherited the money and become rich; hence, by not committing suicide, I contributed causally to becoming rich. I also contributed causally to becoming rich by banking my pay, since this pay (small as it is) constitutes part of my wealth. By definition D3 and axiom A4, I therefore contribute causally to becoming rich in the endeavour to become rich. Since all my endeavours at t are successful, it also follows by definition D6 that my becoming rich is a completely successful intentional action. But this, again, does not seem very plausible.

The two cases just cited raise at least three questions for Chisholm:

1 May we indeed say that in the first case I frightened the burglar *in the endeavour* to do so?
2 May we consider *refraining* from committing suicide something I make happen or contribute causally to obtain by (for example) *not* cutting my own throat?
3 If the cases given are both satisfactory descriptions of completely successful intentional actions, must we not allow that even Chisholm's strong sense of "intentional action" is excessively broad in allowing the possibility of inadvertent success?

My next comment concerns axiom A3, which strikes me as very unconvincing. According to this axiom, if I smile in the endeavour to please you, I contribute causally to this complex state of affairs (of smiling-in-the-endeavour-to-please-you) *in the endeavour* to please you. But this sounds very implausible. I may naturally endeavour to please *myself* by doing something in the endeavour to please you, but it does not seem that my endeavour in doing-something-in-the-endeavour-to-please-you is to please you. To my mind, the most plausible cases of iterated M-statements involve an ultimate endeavour (i.e., an endeavour mentioned by the terminal expression of the M-formula) that is of a higher order than the endeavour mentioned in an earlier part of the formula. Many instances of this kind may be described by saying that in the endeavour to achieve some goal A, one may undertake to bring about a state of affairs B as a means to A. The formula for these plausible instances would be "$M^t(M^tp,q),r$," where "$r \neq q$." If the meaning of the predicate "M^t---, ...$" is such that "$M^t(M^tp,q),q$" *must* be counted true whenever "M^tp,q" is counted true, then its precise interpretation is much less straightforward than what the familiar word "endeavour" naturally suggests.

We might observe in this connection that the significance of axiom A3 is in any case somwhat doubtful in view of axiom A2. Given this latter axiom, iterated M-statements with t constant and only two atomic components p and q are always eliminable in favour of a non-iterated M-statement. The following, in other words, is an immediate consequence of axioms A2 and A3:

TI $M^t(p,q) \equiv M^t(M^tp,q),q$

Since the most plausible cases of iterated M-statements involve a higher-order ultimate endeavour (in the sense already explained), I should prefer to see axiom A3 dropped from the system. What is the point of inferring "$M^t(M^tp,q),q$" from "M^tp,q" when the former is immediately eliminable in favour of the latter? If A3 is dropped, then if there *are* plausible instances of iterated M-formulas in two variables with constant t, they could be asserted on grounds similar to those required for M-statements with more than two atomic components. But perhaps Chisholm has some special reason for maintaining A3. If he has, I should be interested to hear what it is.

I have another puzzle regarding endeavours, this time very complex ones. If $M^t(A,A)$, then doesn't the agent contribute causally to A in the endeavour to contribute causally (i) to do A and (ii) to do *something or other* (perhaps A) in the endeavour to causally contribute to A that does in fact causally contribute to A? This seems in line with Chisholm's intentions, but I am not really sure one way or the other. If the principle is allowed, however, D7 will require amendment.

If $B^t p$, then $M^t p, p$, and then $M^t p$, $[p$ & $(\exists s)\{M^t s, p\}C\{q\}]$. But from $B^t p$ and D7 we may infer $(q)(r)\{\sim M^t r$, $[q$ & $(\exists s)\{M^t s, q\}C\{p\}]\}$, which is incompatible with the principle in question.

The intuitive significance of this case may be brought out as follows. If $B^t p$, must we then *deny* that the agent causally contributed to p for the purpose of contributing causally to p – even when he may so contribute by causing changes in his brain that causally contribute to p? On p. 64 Chisholm says that the statement "At t he makes q happen and his doing so is a basic act" implies "There is no p such that at t he makes p happen for the purpose of making q happen." Should we, or should we not, add to this last sentence the qualification "where p is not equivalent to q"?

We can easily grant that basic acts are not always, or perhaps not even usually, done for a purpose. But need we say that basic acts are *never* done for a purpose – even when the purpose may be nothing more than that of performing those acts? I think not. But perhaps Chisholm will elaborate on this point.

Another puzzle concerns the definitions D4, D5, D6, and D7, for, when interpreted strictly, they imply that one might undertake to make something A contribute causally to something B. But who, really, would actually endeavour to accomplish such a thing? Of whom, that is, would a statement of the form "$M^t p, (\exists s)\{M^t s, p\}C\{q\}$" ever be true? One frequently undertakes to do something A, believing or hoping that A will result in some desired B. But would one ever undertake to make A (or even some event or other) *cause* B? I think not. That to which an *event* (known or unknown) makes a causal contribution is not up to us; we may, given "agent" causation, bring about a certain event, and in doing so we may endeavour to bring about indirectly a further event. But we never, I believe, endeavour to make one thing bring about another. Causal sequences, or natural laws, are like solutions to problems: they are discovered but not made.

My final comment concerns definition D4: $P^t(M^tp,q) =$ Df M^tp, $[p$ & $(\exists r)$ $\{M^tr,p\}C\{q\}]$, where the definiens is interpreted loosely to mean that at t the agent brings it about that p in the endeavour to make it happen (i) that p obtains and (ii) that he does something in endeavouring to bring it about that p that will (as he hopes) bring it about that q. The following case seems to cast doubt on the adequacy of this definition.

At time t I manage to turn on a certain light ($= p$) in the endeavour to do two things: to turn on that light and to contribute causally, by my endeavour to turn it on, to some event or other that will, as I hope, contribute causally to frightening a certain burglar ($= q$). The following, however, is what specifically occurs. In my endeavour to frighten the burglar I reach for what I believe is the chain controlling the light but fall over in the darkness, unwittingly striking the switch that really controls the light, thereby turning on the light. (There is no chain.) I am not only completely unaware that I turned on the light at t, but I even believe it was turned on by my wife, whom I see in the room when the light goes on. In spite of this ignorance on my part, I satisfy the definiens of D7 and can therefore be said to have turned on the light for the purpose of frightening the burglar.

I believe that this case requires some change in D7. The statement "S did A for the purpose of doing B" ought to imply, I believe, that S did not do A inadvertently, unknowingly, accidentally, or by mistake, and also that S's endeavour should concern a particular activity of his (not just some activity or other) by means of which he intends to bring about the desired state of affairs.

Reply

BY RODERICK CHISHOLM

I appreciate the care and attention that Professor Aune has devoted to my paper. His comments are all to the point, and where he has failed to understand me, the fault is mine and not his. He has made clear the need for further explicating certain points and he has formulated several serious objections. I shall discuss: (1) the case of the frightened burglar; (2) the case of the happy depositor; (3) the iterability of "He makes it happen that"; and (4) the limitations of the proposed definition of basic action.

1 The case of the frightened burglar, as Aune indicates, shows the need for being more explicit about the nature of causal contribution. The agent, it will be recalled, was standing in his room thinking and doing so for the purpose of frightening the burglar outside; and the burglar, as it happened, saw him through the window and the appearance of the man was such as to frighten the burglar away. Speaking for the agent, Aune says: "The physiological events I have made happen in my brain contribute causally to my total state at t, and my total state in turn contributes causally to frightening the burglar. By Chisholm's axiom A4 and the transitivity of causal contribution, we may infer that $M'(F,F)$, where 'F' means 'I frighten the burglar.' Assuming that I take no other steps to frighten him at t, we may use definition D7 to infer that $S'IA(F,F)$, which means that I have performed a completely successful intentional act."[1] In short: (i) the agent, by thinking at t, contributed causally to the occurrence in the brain of certain physiological events E; (ii) the occurrence of E contributed causally to the agent's total state at t; (iii) the agent's total state at t contributed causally to the burglar's being frightened; and therefore,

---

[1] It should be noted in passing that, at most, my principles would imply "I made it happen that the burglar was frightened," rather than "I frightened the burglar"; compare footnote 12 of the original paper.

given axiom A4, (iv) the agent by thinking at *t* contributed causally to the frightening of the burglar. But I deny (iii). For the sense of causal contribution with which we are here concerned is *not* one enabling us to say that the agent's total state at *t* contributed causally to the frightening of the burglar.

An alternative reading of "*C* contributes causally to *E*," as I have been using this expression, would be "*C* is a partial cause of *E*." Now it is essential to distinguish "*C* is a partial cause of *E*," or "*C* contributes causally to *E*," from "*C* is a sufficient causal condition of *E*." Oversimplifying slightly, we may say that a set of states of affairs *C* is a *sufficient causal condition* of a set of states of affairs *E*, provided only: no member of *C* begins after the first member of *E* begins; and it is a law of nature, but not a law of logic, that if the members of *C* occur then the members of *E* occur. Ordinarily when we say that one event "causes" another, we do not mean that the one event is a sufficient causal condition, in this sense, of the other. We mean (at least in part) that the one event is a "partial cause" of the other. And an event that is a *partial cause* of another would be any proper subset of a "minimal" sufficient causal condition of the other – where a *minimal sufficient causal condition* of *E* would be (i) a sufficient causal condition of *E*, but (ii) one which has no proper subset that is also a sufficient causal condition of *E*.[2]

But if "*C* contributes causally to *E*" is taken to mean "*C* is a partial cause of *E*," then it is clear that, in the case of the frightened burglar, the agent's *total* state, where this is taken to include the brain events that were caused by his thinking, is not a partial cause of the burglar's being frightened. For it is not a part of any *minimal* sufficient causal condition of the burglar's being frightened.

2 I have made these distinctions in "He Could Have Done Otherwise," *Journal of Philosophy*, 44 (1967), 409–418; see pp. 414–415. A much improved version of that paper may be found in *Philosophy Today No. 1*, edited by Jerry H. Gill (New York: The Macmillan Company, 1968), pp. 236–249.

2 The case of the happy depositor is more difficult to interpret and this is because of the absence of details. It will be recalled that the man refrained from committing suicide and banked his weekly salary in the endeavour to become rich; in so doing, he contributed to his survival; his survival, in turn, contributed to his receiving an inheritance; and the inheritance made him rich. Given my definition of a completely successful action, may we say that the man was completely successful in his endeavour? In other words, was there any state of affairs p which he undertook for the purpose of becoming rich and which was such that he failed to bring p about?

We must distinguish between (a) that act which was the agent's omission of suicide and (b) that act which was the banking of his weekly salary. So far as (a) is concerned, I concede that my account is not adequate to it. For it is not adequate, as it now stands, to those "acts" that are essentially omissions.

So far as (b) is concerned, I think the example suffers because of insufficient detail. Did the agent become rich before the end of the month, and did he bank his salary in the endeavour to bring it about that the interest he would receive at the end of the month would contribute to his becoming rich? In such a case, the receipt of interest, though it would add to his riches, would not contribute to his *becoming* rich. I have the feeling that once the details of the example are worked out, we will find some endeavour that failed – some endeavour that was intended to contribute to the agent's becoming rich and which in fact did not.

3 Aune is disturbed about my A3 and the resulting iteratability of "He contributes causally to its happening that ---." He asks: "What is the point of inferring '$M'(M'p,q),q$' from '$M'p,q$' when the former is immediately eliminable in favour of the latter?" Oversimplifying, we could put the question as: "Why say 'He brings it about that he brings it about that p' if such a statement is immediately eliminable

in favour of 'He brings it about that p'?" I would note two things. The first is that the eliminability of the iterated locution shows it involves no serious disadvantage. And the second is that it has at least one important advantage. Consider the following objection to the view, presupposed here, that an agent is a non-occurrent cause of certain events: "You are committed to saying that some events have no sufficient causal conditions – namely, those events that are caused by agents and not by other events. It is true that you need not say, of such events, that they are 'uncaused' or 'mere chance' events. For you can say that the agent caused them. But what of that event which is the agent's causing such an event? Surely you have to say that *that* is an uncaused or chance event." Given A3, we do not need to say this. For we can say, of that event which was the agent's causing a certain event, that it, too, was caused by the agent.[3]

4 Aune objects to the definition of basic action that I had proposed. According to the definition, in effect, the agent performs so-and-so as a basic act at t, provided that he brings about so-and-so intentionally at t, and provided further that there is nothing he undertakes at t for the purpose of bringing so-and-so about. Aune writes: "We can easily grant that basic acts are not always, or perhaps not even usually, done for a purpose. But need we say that basic acts are *never* done for a purpose – even when the purpose may be nothing more than

---

3 I would say, in answer to one of Aune's questions, that the present view does imply that "the person actually *initiates* a causal sequence." I would agree with Prichard's suggestion that we must distinguish between those things that a man makes happen directly and those things he makes happen, but not directly; see H. A. Prichard, *Moral Obligation* (Oxford: The Clarendon Press, 1962), p. 193. (We could say that a man makes something p happen *directly* provided he makes p happen, and there is no q such that he makes q happen, and q's happening contributes causally to p's happening.) Aune says that "if physiology tells us that a man's actions are caused by physiological changes, it equally tells us that these physiological changes are caused by further physiological changes." But there is a certain ambiguity in the statement that physiology "tells us" this. It may be that certain physiologists have *said* this. But are there any physiologists who have *shown* that it is true, or who *know* that it is true?

that of performing those acts? I think not." But the definition does not imply that, if performing so-and-so is a basic act, then the agent had *no purpose in performing so-and-so*; it implies rather that, if performing so-and-so is a basic act at *t*, then there is nothing that the agent brought about at *t for the purpose of performing so-and-so*.

Nevertheless, I believe that the definition of basic act should be revised, for the present definition is overly restrictive. Thus a man might raise his arm a foot above his head for the purpose of getting it more than an inch above his head; and getting it more than an inch above his head, in this situation, would seem to be a basic act even though there was some other thing that he did for the purpose of getting it done. I think, therefore, the definition should be revised in the following way. We will say that the agent performs so-and-so as a basic act, provided that he intentionally makes so-and-so happen and that any state of affairs he makes happen for the purpose of making so-and-so happen is a state of affairs that entails so-and-so. Expressing "entails," once again, by means of the arrow "→," we would have:

$$B^t(\text{---}) = \text{Df } IA^t(\text{---}) \ \& \ (p)[P^t(U^t p, \text{---}) \supset (p \rightarrow \text{---})]$$

The revised definition will not revive any of the puzzles that were dealt with in the original paper.

3 / Wanting: Some Pitfalls

R. M. Hare

The first part of this paper is an attempt to find a hole in Professor Max Black's argument in his article "The Gap between 'Is' and 'Should.' "[1] Let me start with a concrete example. Uncle John, an elderly and rich bachelor, and his nephew and sole heir, James, are fishing from a small boat in shark-infested waters out of sight of other vessels. As they are waiting for a bite, James says:

JAMES Do you know, there's nothing in the world I want more than to have half a million dollars, and spend it on enjoying myself.

UNCLE JOHN I suppose that's true. You could never do without women, and women are expensive these days. Besides, if you say that that's what you want, who am I to doubt your word? You have certainly been trying very hard lately to make money at the races, but you haven't had any luck.

JAMES Yes; repeated failures in that and other directions have convinced me that the one and only way of getting half a million dollars is to push you out of the boat.

1 Max Black, "The Gap between 'Is' and 'Should,' " *Philosophical Review*, 73 (1964), 165–181. If, in the course of arguing that Black's inference schema is *invalid*, I suggest that certain other schemata are, by contrast, *valid*, I do so without confidence, and only because their plausibility, and their deceptive similarity to Black's schema, may explain why he thought his valid. Professor Gauthier has half-convinced me that they are invalid also.

UNCLE JOHN I'm afraid you're right about that. You never were much good at honest toil.

JAMES So you agree that I do want half a million dollars, and that the only way of getting them is to push you out of the boat. What do you think I should do, then?

UNCLE JOHN Well, since you want, more than anything else, to have half a million dollars, and since the one and only way of getting them is to push me out of the boat, I can only conclude that you should push me out of the boat.

JAMES I quite agree with both your premises and your reasoning; therefore, since I never disregard soundly-based advice, especially from uncles ...

(pushes Uncle John out of boat)

Now it seems obvious that there is something logically wrong, and not merely morally disreputable, about this dialogue. But *what* is wrong with it is not easy to say. Let me first reject some suggestions which I think do not go to the root of the matter. First, I would agree, if anybody wanted me to for the sake of argument, that it would make no difference whether the word "should" were used in the dialogue or the word "ought." Second, our unease has nothing to do with any *moral* feelings we have about pushing people out of boats; neither party to the dialogue says anything relevant about morals, and we may suppose that Uncle John's natural aversion to being fed to the sharks has other sources than moral disapproval of murder. Morals just do not come into the matter; we should still find the argument odd even if we and both parties were quite amoral.

Third, the argument is not odd because James must be presumed to have other higher or preferred ends which conflict with his attaining his half-million dollars by this means. He said, you remember, "There's nothing I want more." And fourth, Uncle John could not have escaped from the argument by withdrawing from the advising role; for he was asked a straight question, "What do you think I should do then?" If the conclusion follows from the premises, he must give the answer he did.

I think, therefore, that we shall have to investigate the matter a bit more deeply. It may help us if we consider and contrast the following two remarks, both of which might be made to a friend dining in a restaurant:

1 If you want sugar in your soup, you should ask the waiter.
2 If you want sugar in your soup, you should get tested for diabetes.

The difference between the two remarks can be brought out, first, by noticing the entirely different grounds that would be given to justify them. The first would be justified by pointing out that the waiter has the only access to sugar. The second would be justified by arguing that an inordinate desire for sugar is a symptom of diabetes, and that those with diabetes should have it treated. Alternatively, we might bring out the difference in the following way: the first suggests that asking the waiter would be a means to having sugar in one's soup; the second does not suggest that getting tested for diabetes is a means to having sugar in one's soup.

The difference between these two kinds of "If you want" statements was pointed out by me in *The Language of Morals*,[2] and also by Jonathan Harrison,[3] who made the additional point that the consequent of the "diabetes" hypothetical can be detached by using *modus ponens*, but that that of the "waiter" hypothetical cannot. Thus, it is permissible to argue "If you want sugar in your soup, you should get tested for diabetes; but you do want sugar in your soup; therefore you should (absolutely) get tested for diabetes." But it is not permissible to argue "If you want sugar in your soup, you should ask the waiter; but you do want sugar in your soup; therefore you should (absolutely) ask the waiter." As we shall see in more detail later, that is what is wrong, both with the

2 R. M. Hare, *The Language of Morals* (Oxford: The Clarendon Press, 1952), pp. 34ff.
3 *Aristotelian Society Supplement*, 28 (1954), 111–134.

James–Uncle John dialogue, and with Max Black's article on which it is modelled. I say "you should (absolutely)" in order to contrast it with "you should, if you want sugar in your soup."

Let us consider the meaning of "If you want" in the two cases. In the "diabetes" case, a first approximation would be to say that it means the same as "If you, as a matter of psychological fact, have a desire." I am very much inclined to deny that it means anything like this in the "waiter" case. But we cannot clarify this question until we know more about what it is to have a desire. Mr. Kenny has suggested, adopting a device of Professor Geach's, that to have a desire is to say-in-one's-heart an imperative.[4] This is, of course, artificial, and I do not in any case have to take over the suggestion in its entirety. Neither Kenny nor Geach, I think, wishes to suggest that thinking is subvocal mouthing. Their suggestion, though artificial, is illuminating, and its artificiality is, perhaps, no greater than that which we have to endure in all cases in which we want to give linguistic expression to something that we do not say but only think.

Thus, I may be thinking that the clock has just struck five, but may *say* nothing, either out loud, or even subvocally. It is useful, indeed essential, to be able to isolate the *proposition* which expresses what I am thinking, or would express it if it were uttered. It may be going too far to say that this kind of thought cannot be had at all by a creature which could not in principle express it in words; but at any rate, if we want to display the logical relations between this thought and other thoughts, we cannot do so without first putting them into words. Thus, if I not only think that the clock has just struck five, but think that for that reason it must be just after five, because the clock strikes five at five o'clock only, the logic of my reasoning cannot be displayed without putting the propositions (premises and conclusion) into words.

4 Anthony Kenny, *Action, Emotion and Will* (London: Routledge & Kegan Paul, 1963), Chs. 10 and 11.

It is this second point which is most relevant to the case of practical inferences. Unless we make some such move as Kenny's, we shall not be able to display the logical relations between desires and other thoughts or expressions. Many people who have written on this subject have thought that the way to get desires into the logical machinery was to put in premisses of the form "*X* wants (or desires) that *p*." But this is as unpromising a move as it would be to try to set up the propositional calculus, operating, not with propositions like "*p*," "*q*," and "*r*," but with propositions like "*X* believes that *p*," etc. On Kenny's view, "*X* wants sugar in his soup" is to be rendered "*X* says in his heart 'Let me have sugar in my soup.' " We do not need, however, to employ quotation marks, which may seem objectionable, as suggesting subvocal speech. We can say, "*X* wants that he have (note the mood) sugar in his soup." Here the subordinate *oratio-obliqua* clause "that he have sugar in his soup" stands for what in *oratio recta* would be an imperative; if we were translating "wants that he have sugar in his soup" into Urdu, the construction used would be that appropriate to an indirect command. And indeed, in Urdu, as in English, if we are reporting in indirect speech a command given by somebody else, we may say to the person commanded "So and so *wants* you to do such and such." So there is good reason for allowing that, whether or not the man who wants something "says anything in his heart," an appropriate expression in language for what he is thinking, if we are to have one, is an imperative.

Now let us consider the "diabetes" example with this point in mind. The inference seems to go like this (if you will tolerate for the moment Kenny's artificial translation): If anyone does as a matter of fact say-in-his-heart "Let me have sugar in my soup," he should get tested for diabetes; but *X* (the man in question) does, as a matter of fact, say-in-his-heart "Let me have sugar in my soup"; therefore *X* should get tested for diabetes. This is relatively unproblematical. It is the actual occurrence, in fact, of this thought in his heart which entitles us to detach the consequent of the hypothetical. But when we come to the "waiter" example, the situation is different. There, what entitles us to detach the consequent is not the mere fact of X's saying-in-his-heart "Let me have sugar in my soup." Before we can *ourselves* affirm absolutely "X should ask the waiter," *we* have to be, like X, saying-in-our-hearts "Let X have sugar in his soup." In fact, the real premiss in the argument is not the factual statement that X wants, or says-in-his-heart, what he wants or says; the real premiss is *what* he is saying in his heart – the thought that he is having, not the fact that he is having it. From this it follows that the consequent of a "waiter" type of hypothetical "should"-statement is detachable only by someone who is prepared himself to subscribe to the imperative which is implicitly contained in the conditional clause.

There is a subsidiary difficulty here which I am not going to try to deal with. Clearly there is a difference between the two utterances, "If you want sugar in your soup, *you should ask* the waiter," and "If you want sugar in your soup, *ask* the waiter." This difference has something to do with the universalizability of hypothetical "ought"- and "should"-statements; but I am not able to clarify it at the moment. However, I think that we are now in a position to explain both the plausibility of Max Black's argument and the strangeness of the Uncle John dialogue which is of the same form.

The plausibility of this form of argument (provided that the right instances are chosen for illustrating it), stems from the fact that it is easy to insert into it a step consisting of a proposition which seems to be both analytically true and sufficient to guarantee the validity of the argument. Black's example is:

Fischer wants to mate Botwinnik;

The one and only way to mate Botwinnik is for Fischer to move the Queen;

Therefore Fischer should move the Queen.

Into this argument we might insert the apparently analytic step:

A If the one and only way to mate Botwinnik is for Fischer to move the Queen, then, if Fischer wants to mate Botwinnik, he should move the Queen.

This might be thought to be merely a particular case of the general analytic truth:

A′ If the one and only way to achieve a certain end is to adopt a certain means, then, if anybody wants to achieve the end, he should adopt the means.

This is, however, one of Satan's cleverest sophisms, and many there be who have gone to Hell through being beguiled by it – like James in the dialogue. For the sense in which this is analytic is the sense which makes the second half of it ("if anybody wants to achieve the end, he should adopt the means") analogous to the "waiter" hypothetical. In this sense, it is a complete justification of the proposition that if anybody wants *E* he should do *M*, to say that *M* is the only way of achieving *E*. But in *this* sense the consequent is not detachable. In order to make it detachable, we have to take "if anybody wants to achieve the end, he should adopt the means" in a sense analogous to that of the "diabetes" hypothetical. This is the sense we have to give the words, therefore, if we want to make the conclusion "Therefore Fischer should move the Queen" a valid conclusion from the premisses

Fischer wants to mate Botwinnik

and

If Fischer wants to mate Botwinnik, he should move the Queen.

But in *this* sense neither A nor A′ are analytic. The Fischer-Botwinnik argument, therefore, has a premiss which is not only suppressed but equivocal; taken one way, it is analytic and hardly needs stating, but is insufficient to validate the argument; taken the other way, it validates the argument, but is not analytic.

The consequent of a "waiter" type of hypothetical is detachable by putting in an *imperative* premiss. In the Uncle John case, this would be of the form "Let James have half a million dollars"; in the Fischer-Botwinnik case it would be of the form "Let Fischer mate Botwinnik." It is because Uncle John obviously would not (in the circumstances) assent to this imperative premiss that the dialogue with which I started seemed so strange. It is because Uncle John does not want, more than anything else (even his own survival), that James should have half a million dollars, that he has not really got the logical wherewithal to enable him to detach the consequent which says that James should push him out of the boat. The *statement* that *James* wants this is not enough. For what would really make possible the detachment of the consequent is not *the fact that* James says-in-his-heart "Let me have half a million dollars," but the thing that he says in his heart. Uncle John has to say this thing in his own heart before the *modus ponens* machinery will operate for him – for nobody can be compelled to assent to the conclusion of even a valid inference unless he accepts all its premisses.

But, it may be objected, is this true of the Fischer-Botwinnik inference? Has the speaker of this inference got to assent himself to the imperative which is being assented to or said-in-his-heart by Fischer when he wants to mate Botwinnik? I would answer, "In a manner of speaking, yes." Suppose that a spectator of the game very much wants Fischer not to move the Queen (perhaps he has a large bet on what Fischer's next move will be). He can follow this strategy:

1 He assents to "If Fischer wants to mate Botwinnik he should move the Queen" only in the "waiter" sense (which is the only sense in which he can be compelled to accept it, given that the one and only way, etc.).

2 He then refuses to accept the imperative premiss which, on this interpretation, is needed to detach the consequent "Fischer should move the Queen." This premiss is "Let Fischer mate Botwinnik."

No doubt this spectator could be compelled to assent to the conclusion "Fischer should move the Queen" in the sense in which it is elliptical for "If Fischer wants to mate Botwinnik, he should move the Queen" (taken in the "waiter" sense). But in that case he would have assented only to a covertly hypothetical "should," not to a categorical one. I do not think that many people would wish to deny that hypothetical "should"-statements can be derived from "is"-statements. It is the categorical "should"-conclusion that is the real quarry; and that has escaped. And I may add in passing that, even if Black had caught his quarry in the Fischer-Botwinnik case, he would be very far from having proved the validity of the inference about pain which he inserts right at the end of his article. But that is another story.

I have, in the above, made some use of Kenny's idea that to have a desire is to say something (namely an imperative) "in one's heart." I am not committing myself to Kenny's account of wanting or of intention in its entirety. What I have said is that if we are going to talk about the logical relations between intentions or between wishes in the same sort of way as we sometimes do talk about the logical relations between beliefs, it is necessary to have a form of words which expresses the intention or the wish, or at any rate expresses it *if* it is expressed; and that the imperative sentence is a suitable form of words. I may remark in passing that, if we do express wishes in words, this enables us to distinguish between two sorts of wishes which do need distinguishing, namely those which are naturally expressed in the imperative, and those which are naturally expressed in various "optative"

D

constructions (e.g., "Would that I were a bird!"). This supports Miss Anscombe's distinction[5] between the kind of wanting of which "the primitive sign is trying to get," and "idle wishing." We might say that the latter is idle, unlike the former, because its expression, unlike an imperative, does not command any action.

Just as two beliefs are mutually inconsistent if their expressions in statements would be mutually inconsistent, so two desires are mutually inconsistent if their expressions in the imperative mood would be mutually inconsistent. I cannot rationally think that p and that not p, because "p and not p" is self-contradictory; and I cannot rationally want (in the non-idle sense) that p and that not p, because the command that p and not p is self-contradictory. And just as we could not account for the mutual inconsistency of the beliefs that p and that not p by saying that "x believes that p and x believes that not p" is self-contradictory (for it is not), so we cannot account for the mutual inconsistency of the desires that p and that not p by saying that "x wants that p and x wants that not p" is self-contradictory; for that is not self-contradictory either.

There is, of course, a tiresome problem about the relations between the desire that p, which is not a speech-act, and the expressed command or request that p, which is. However, I do not feel called upon to say anything about this problem, because it is a quite general problem about the relations between thought and speech, affecting assertions and commands alike. This might be the subject of another paper, but I shall not attempt to deal with it in this one. I do not see that there is here any problem peculiar to imperative speech-acts. However, since I am advocating an account of the relation between desires and their expression in language which owes something to Kenny's, though it is not identical with his, it is perhaps apposite to say something in answer

5 G. E. M. Anscombe, *Intention*, 2nd ed. (Oxford: Blackwell, 1957), pp. 66f.

to various objections which have been made against Kenny's account, whether or not my own is exposed to them.

The first objection I wish to consider is made by Mr. Pears.[6] He is criticizing the view that *intentions* are the sayings-in-the-heart of commands. There are, of course, important differences between desires and intentions, and it is not to be assumed that what can be said of one can be said of the other. Nevertheless, Pears's criticism of this theory is worth examining. He puts the theory he is attacking in the following form: " 'I intend to do *A*,' when it is a genuine report of a state of mind, is tantamount to the statement 'I have said in my heart, "Let me do *A*." ' " This is not a very fair statement of the theory, for it exposes it gratuitously to the objection that a man might have said in his heart "Let me do *A*," and then, afterwards, changed his mind and said (also in his heart) "No, let me not do *A* after all." Such a man would have said in his heart "Let me do *A*," but would not now intend to do *A*. However, let us ignore this complication, and suppose that the theory is not what Pears says it is, but rather, that the man who intends to do *A* is the man who in his heart *subscribes* (not necessarily subvocally and not necessarily occurrently) to the command "Let me do *A*."

Pears says of the theory "The kind of command that is meant must be self-exhortation." It is not clear to me why he says this, for he gives no reasons. Since the brunt of his subsequent argument against the theory depends on its being this particular kind of command that is in question, he surely owed it to Kenny to justify his choice of this implausible candidate. Exhortation is in fact a rather special use of the imperative mood. As Pears says "To exhort oneself to do something is a way of getting oneself to decide to do it." This statement, which might be generalized to cover all exhortations and not just self-addressed ones, is another way

6 D. F. Pears, "Predicting and Deciding," *Proceedings of the British Academy* (1964), pp. 203f.

of putting the point that an exhortation is, in Austin's term, at least partly a perlocutionary act. I say "at least partly," because it might plausibly be maintained that an exhortation is also an illocutionary act; for the man who says "I exhort you to do *A*" seems to be performing (at least as part of what he does) an illocutionary act of the same genus as that which includes requesting, ordering, and praying – i.e., the genus of speech-acts that are typically done in the imperative mood.

It seems to me to be a mistake, however, to suppose that *all* speech-acts of this genus are also, essentially, perlocutionary acts, even in part. It is certainly extremely common to find philosophers saying that commands are, essentially, ways of *getting* people to do things. Professor Black even refers to them as verbal prods or pushes.[7] But the philosophers who say this sort of thing usually do so because they have not sufficiently studied Austin's distinction; and this cannot be true of Pears.

That a command is not essentially – though it may be commonly – a way of getting people to do things, was argued by me at some length in a paper a long time ago.[8] I think that I was there making in other words the same distinction as Austin called the illocutionary-perlocutionary distinction. On one of the very few occasions on which he read a paper in public about this distinction (at a colloquium organized by the British Council in Oxford in 1955), Austin was kind enough to say that he was saying the same sort of thing as I had been saying, and I think it was to this article he was referring. Neither as I made it, nor as he made it, is it free from difficulties, and there are annoying overlapping cases, of which exhorting is one and warning is another, which will continue to give trouble until we are a lot clearer about the basis of the distinction.

However, it ought to be clear at least that it is not true

7 Black, "The Gap between 'Is' and 'Should,' " pp. 172f.
8 R. M. Hare, "The Freedom of the Will," *Aristotelian Society Supplement*, 25 (1951), 201.

of commands in general that the person who issues them is, *ex vi termini*, trying to get people to do the things specified. The sadistic schoolmaster, who commands his boys to keep silent in the hope that this will cause them to talk so that he can beat them, is still commanding or telling them to keep quiet. Even if, as Miss Anscombe thinks and as I agree, "the primitive sign of wanting is trying to get," and even if, as Kenny argued, wanting is to be represented as saying-in-the-heart an imperative, it does not follow that imperatives themselves are to be defined as verbal attempts to get. The man who wants that p says in his heart (on this view) "Let it be the case that p"; and if this is what he is really saying in his heart, he *will* try to bring it about that p. But the saying of the imperative is not itself, essentially, an attempt to bring it about that p. How could it be, if the saying is only in the heart, and p is some external event like being given a drink?

Coming back, however, to the case of intending, with which we are at present concerned, it seems clear that if Kenny were to choose, not exhortation, but some other kind of command, as the kind that is being said in the heart when a man forms an intention, he would escape Pears's objection. This is stated as follows: "To exhort oneself to do something is a way of getting oneself to decide to do it, or else a way of keeping oneself up to the mark after one has decided to do it: to form an intention is neither of these things."[9] This seems to me true; it is at any rate not far from the truth to say that forming an intention and deciding are the same thing; and therefore, if exhorting oneself is a different thing from deciding, it must be a different thing from forming an intention. But the argument touches Kenny no more than it would touch somebody who maintained the surely irrefutable thesis that when Hannibal orders his troops to march on Rome he is commanding them to march on Rome. Here, too, if we made the gratuitous assumption that the kind of command that is meant "must be" exhortation, we could argue that ordering

9 Pears, "Predicting and Deciding," p. 207.

cannot be this kind of commanding and therefore (on this assumption) cannot be any kind of commanding, because to exhort is different from ordering.

That exhorting and ordering are different could easily be shown. Hannibal might first order his troops to march, and then, in an effort to get them to carry out his orders, exhort them to march. Or, if they were well-disciplined and did not need exhorting, he might just order and not exhort them. If, on the other hand, they were so mutinous that an order from him would be the very thing that would stop them marching, he might refrain from ordering them but just exhort them – perhaps enlarging on the beauties of the Roman women. If we found such a scandalous inducement reported in Livy prefaced by the words "*hortatus est*," we should not be surprised. But the distinctness of ordering from exhorting does nothing to establish the distinctness of ordering from commanding, unless the assumption is made that "the kind of command that is meant must be exhortation."

The point is that commanding and ordering are illocutionary acts, but exhorting is, essentially, at least partly a perlocutionary act – an act of trying to get. Therefore the illocutionary act of ordering or in general of commanding is separable from the perlocutionary act of exhorting. So to prove that intending is not self-exhortation is not to prove that it is not self-commanding.

Actually it is very plausible to say that when Hannibal orders his troops to march on Rome he is not merely commanding them to do so, but expressing the intention that they should do so; and this lends some plausibility to the thesis that when I form the intention to go to Rome, I have that in my mind which would, if expressed in words, naturally be expressed by saying "Let me go to Rome," or, if I were to address myself in military style in the mood which I was taught in the Army to call the future imperative, "Hare will go to Rome," or "I will go to Rome."

Though it is easy to see why Pears thought his argument

cogent, given that he thought that the self-addressed command in question was a perlocutionary act, it is not so easy to account for his adopting the following subsidiary argument. He says: "Conveying information is not the primary purpose of self-exhortation, whereas it is the primary purpose of the two utterances ['I will do A' and 'I intend to do A']."[10] It seems to me that this lacks at any rate the appearance of cogency as an argument against Kenny's view; for on Kenny's view "I intend to do A" *would* have the primary purpose of informing (viz., of the fact that I subscribe to the self-addressed command to do A); and, on the other hand, "I will do A," which is on Kenny's view not primarily informative, is *indeed* not primarily informative, but rather an expression of an intention or resolve. So Kenny, at least as far as concerns the primary informative purpose, or lack of it, of these two utterances, gets it right both times. Pears, on the other hand, seems to think that they are both primarily informative – which is false; and he seems to think – which is also false – that Kenny is required by his view to say that they are both primarily non-informative.

I have already touched on the fact that there are different sorts of commands, in the generic sense of that term; and I must now say more about this in order to counter one of several objections made by Mr. D. R. Bell[11] against Kenny's views and my own. In the ordinary sense, commands, like orders (which are not the same thing) are distinguished from requests and prayers and other species of the genus to which they all belong, namely the genus of speech-acts typically expressed in the imperative mood. This, I say, is the ordinary sense of the word "command." If I *ask* you to shut the door, I am not, in this ordinary sense, giving you a command. Now we do not have, in ordinary untechnical English, a single word for the genus I have just mentioned (though we have

10 *Ibid.*, pp. 207f.
11 D. R. Bell, "Imperatives and the Will," *Proceedings of the Aristotelian Society*, 66 (1965–66), 129.

a generic *verb* for these speech-acts, namely "tell to"). I now like to use the word "imperation" for the genus of "tellings to," meaning, roughly, "speech-act for which an imperative is a natural form." But in the traditional grammar-books we find the word "command" used generically in this sense. For example, if I had to translate into Latin either the sentence "He ordered his troops to pursue the enemy," or the sentence "He begged her to stay," or the sentence "He prayed to God to save him," I should in all these cases use one of the constructions which you will find classified in Kennedy's Latin Primer as "indirect commands." Having been brought up on this excellent book, I thought that it would be sufficient, when using the word "command" for the genus in my book, *The Language of Morals*, simply to spend one paragraph at the beginning of the book making this clear.

I did not, however, succeed in making it clear to Mr. Bell; for, although he quotes from this very paragraph, he does not quote the sentence in which I say that I am going to use the word "command" generically like the grammarians, but proceeds to take "command" in the sense of "order" in expounding and attacking my views. He does the same to Kenny, who has also done his best to make himself clear. Bell therefore spoils a promising article by attacking a nonexistent target who thinks that intentions are self-addressed orders. Since he also makes the mistake mentioned above of interpreting orders as attempts to get something done (a view which he curiously attributes to Austin), he is evidently in some confusion about Austin's illocutionary-perlocutionary distinction. He even at one point, within three lines, says that orders are *il*locutionary acts and have the function of getting something done.[12]

Those of Bell's objections to Kenny and myself which are not vitiated by the above confusions take the form of alleged vicious regresses. There are two of these, so similar that it is hard to tell them apart. One of them goes: if the performance

12 *Ibid.*, pp. 140f.

of a voluntary act involves addressing an order to oneself, then this in turn, being also a voluntary act, involves addressing to oneself an order to address the order, and so on. The other goes: if intending an act is addressing to oneself an order, then if obeying the order is also a voluntary act, there must also be an order, addressed to oneself, to obey the order, and so on. That these regresses (if they are really more than one) are spurious is indicated by the fact that they can be generated without bringing in the "Imperative Theory of the Will" or referring to "orders" at all, simply by using the words "intend" or "form an intention" themselves. Thus: (1) if the performance of a voluntary act involves forming an intention, then this in turn, being also a voluntary act, involves forming an intention to form the intention, and so on; (2) if intending an act involves forming an intention, then, if carrying out the intention is also a voluntary act, the agent has to form a second intention to carry out the first intention, and so on. It is not incumbent upon me to solve either of these regresses, since they arise independently of my views; they do not look too difficult to solve, but I shall be interested to hear people's views on them.

I will sum up this somewhat loosely knit paper by merely listing the pitfalls which I have been trying to mark. There is first of all the mistake of supposing that we can establish the statement "I want to do *A*" as if it were a *statement about* a desire, but then using it as a premiss of inferences as if it were an *expression of* a desire (a role more naturally performed by an imperative); second, there is the confusion between commands as a genus and commands as a species of that genus; third, there is the assumption that commands are essentially perlocutionary acts; fourth, there is the refusal to allow liberties, in speaking of mental imperative "speech-acts," that most of us allow in speaking of mental indicative "speech-acts." This last pitfall I merely marked and did not discuss.

Comments

BY DAVID GAUTHIER

I

In this paper Professor Hare's primary concern is with the role of wanting in practical reasoning. His positive thesis I take to be twofold: (a) it is appropriate to express wants as imperatives (commands, imperations); (b) it is wants, expressed as imperatives, which are required as premisses in practical inferences.

The second part of his paper is concerned, if somewhat indirectly, with a defence of (a). I can find little positive argument to support it. However, Hare does show that certain counter-arguments are fallacious, because they confuse the genus imperative with the species hortative (Pears) or command (Bell). I agree that those criticized do confuse certain species of speech-acts with a genus, but whether this is so or not, I am sure that Mr. Pears will defend himself more ably than I could, were I to try. I shall therefore try to show that (a) is mistaken, in selecting the wrong genus of speech-act for the expression of wants.

The first part of Hare's paper is concerned with (b) – that wants, expressed as imperatives, are required as premisses of practical inferences. This thesis is used to defend the position that a categorical "should"-statement cannot be derived from an "is"-statement. Again I find little positive argument, but rather a rebuttal of Max Black's attempt to derive "should"-statements from statements *about* wants, which are "is"-statements. Once more I agree that the position criticized is mistaken. But I shall try to show that the debate between Hare and Black is largely irrelevant to the question whether "should"-statements may be derived from "is"-statements, because neither Hare nor Black distinguishes two utterly different types of inference, both of which might be called practical. Let me hasten to add that my own previous sallies in discussing practical reasoning have been equally undiscriminating.

II

I shall now try to construct an example to suggest that Hare's position is as unsatisfactory as Black's. Tom and Jane are at the football game, championing the University of Toronto against the University of Western Ontario. With Toronto leading 17–14, in the closing seconds Western attempts a desperation pass, which to the anguish of Tom and Jane is caught by Smith in the Toronto end-zone for a touchdown. The following unlikely conversation ensues:

TOM Smith shouldn't have caught that pass.

JANE I agree that it's an awful shame he caught it. But why ever shouldn't he have? After all, he was trying to win for Western.

TOM I know. But I wanted Toronto to win, not Western.

JANE Of course, but what's that got to do with it? Look. Smith wanted Western to win. The one and only way for Western to win was for him to catch the pass. So he should have caught it.

TOM You can't detach the conclusion of that argument. I agree that if Smith wanted Western to win, then he should have caught the pass. And of course he did want Western to win. But you can't conclude that *categorically* he should have caught the pass. To do so you must accept the imperative premiss "Let Western win." But we accept the premiss "Let Toronto win." The one and only way for Toronto to have won was for Smith not to have caught the pass. So we can detach the conclusion from "If we wanted Toronto to win, Smith shouldn't have caught the pass," and assert categorically that Smith shouldn't have caught the pass.

Tom's final remarks may be on shaky ground since he has

not read about universalizability. But it seems clear that something more has gone wrong here, and that Tom's willingness or unwillingness to assent to "Let Western win" is utterly irrelevant to whether he should or should not assert categorically that Smith should have caught the pass. Tom's argument against asserting the conclusion is logically out of place, and not merely poor sportsmanship.

The relation of this example to Black's Fischer-Botwinnik case is, I hope, clear. Whether or not the spectator is disposed to assent to "Let Fischer win" is quite irrelevant to whether or not he should assert "Fischer should move the Queen." Indeed it seems to me that "Fischer should move the Queen" is adequately supported (though not entailed) by the premisses Black provides. It also seems to me that "James should push Uncle John out of the boat" is not adequately supported (much less entailed) by the formally similar premisses Hare provides. To see what has gone wrong, with both Black and Hare, we must reconsider the nature of practical inference.

III

In his article "Practical Inference"[1] von Wright proposes the following primary inference pattern:[2]

> *A* wants to attain *x*.
> Unless *A* does *y*, he will not attain *x*.
> Therefore *A* must do *y*.

Von Wright notes that first person inferences conforming to this pattern are very different from third person inferences. "In the case of the inference in the first person ... the premises are a person's *want* and his *state of knowing or*

---

1 Georg Henrik von Wright, "Practical Inference," *The Philosophical Review*, 72 (1963), 159–179.
2 *Ibid.*, p. 172.

believing a certain condition to be necessary for the fulfillment of that want. The conclusion is an *act*, something that this person does."[3] On the other hand, "In the case of the inference in the third person ... the premises are the *propositions* that a certain person pursues a certain end of action and that a certain thing is a necessary means to this end. The conclusion is a third proposition, namely that the person will fail to reach some end of his action unless he does this thing."[4] Note that for inferences on this pattern, there is no question of requiring the reasoner to express his own want, or to assent to the agent's want, unless he is himself the agent. Thus it would seem that we can construct practical inferences taking as premises both those given by Black in the Fischer-Botwinnik example, and those given by Hare in the Uncle John and James example.

What is the status of the conclusion in such an inference? Von Wright claims that " 'Must' is somehow stronger than 'ought.' "[5] Thus it would seem that the conclusion is a very strong normative judgment. And Hare would no doubt object that such a conclusion cannot be derived from factual premises, such as von Wright provides.

But this interpretation is misleading. Von Wright is not concerned with categorical normative judgments, but with judgments which express practical necessity.[6] The conclusion states what the agent must do, or the conclusion is the agent's doing what he must do, *in order to* attain the end given in the premisses. The conclusion is detachable, but not as a normative judgment about what the agent should or ought to do.

Black's confusion should now be clear. He has failed to distinguish practical inference of the type discussed by von Wright from that of concern to Hare. From "Fischer wants to mate Botwinnik" and "Unless Fischer moves the Queen, he will not mate Botwinnik," we may derive "Fischer must

3 *Ibid.*, pp. 168–169.
4 *Ibid.*, p. 168.
5 *Ibid.*, p. 161.
6 *Ibid.*, pp. 165–166.

move the Queen," but not "Fischer should move the Queen." And from "James wants half a million dollars" and "Unless James pushes Uncle John out of the boat he will not obtain half a million dollars," we may derive "James must push Uncle John out of the boat," but not "James should push Uncle John out of the boat." Uncle John can point out to James that, given what James wants, there is an objective practical necessity that James push Uncle John out of the boat, without advising James so to act. For Uncle John may not believe that James should do what he most wants.

But Hare has equally failed to distinguish two types of practical inference. From "Let me (Fischer) mate Botwinnik" interpreted as an expression of Fischer's want, we may derive "I (Fischer) must move the Queen," but not "I should move the Queen." Just as Black is mistaken in supposing that "should"-statements may be derived from statements of wants, so – I shall argue – Hare is mistaken in supposing that "should"-statements may be derived from expressions of wants. Black has confused von Wright's practical inference in the third person with inference to "should"-statements. Hare has confused von Wright's practical inference in the first person with inference to "should"-statements.

IV

As a first step in my attempt to demonstrate Hare's confusion, I shall consider briefly how wants may be appropriately expressed – or in other words, I shall consider the imperative theory of the will.

I propose to substitute "*A* would attain *x*" for "*A* wants to attain *x*" in von Wright's inference pattern. This clarifies the status of the expression, for in the third person "He would attain *x*" is naturally taken as a statement *about* the agent and his want, but in the first person "I would attain *x*" is naturally taken as an expression of the agent's want. Thus "I would attain x" corresponds to Hare's "Let me attain x"; "He would attain x" corresponds to Black's "He wants to attain x."

But now I want to claim that "I would attain x" is not an imperative expression. Yet it is a much more natural way of expressing one's want, than Hare's invented formula "Let me attain x."

If "I would attain x" were an imperative, of what species would it be? I have identified five main species of imperative – command, instruction, recommendation, hortation, and request. Hare rightly insists that expressions of one's wants are neither commands nor hortations; unfortunately, it is even more evident that they are not instructions, nor recommendations, nor requests.

A defender of the imperative theory might propose that expressions of want and will constitute a quite distinctive species of imperative. But I am unable to see what they have in common with other imperatives, and I do believe that they lend themselves to quite another classification. This is suggested by the expression "I would attain x," which is neither indicative nor imperative, but optative.

Now it is true that expressions of wants are not expressions of wishes, and that, as Hare has pointed out, wishes are expressed by optatives ("Would that I were rich!"). But it would be the same *non sequitur* criticized by Hare in Pears and Bell to argue that therefore expressions of wants are not optatives. There are different species of optative – expressions of wish ("Would that ..."), of want ("I would ..."), and of intention ("I will ...") are three such species.

V

The type of practical inference exemplified in the inference pattern given by von Wright I propose to call *optative inference*. I shall reformulate the pattern in this way:

A would attain *x*.
Unless *A* does *y*, he will not attain *x*.
Therefore *A* needs to do *y*.

I replace "must" by "needs to" in the conclusion, to clarify the type of practical necessity it states. "Must" may be taken as categorical; "needs to" indicates dependence on certain (unspecified) conditions. And "needs to" avoids all suggestion of a normative judgment about what *A* should do.

In a first person optative inference, the initial premiss expresses a want, and the conclusion an action. In a third person optative inference, the first premiss states what the agent wants, and the conclusion states what is needful for its attainment.

Optative inference is surely what Aristotle intended in his discussion of the practical syllogism. It is reasoning which is most directly connected *with* action. But it is not reasoning *about* action. The conclusion is not a practical judgment, or judgment of what it is reasonable to do. Thus the conclusion of an optative inference has no *normative* force.

But the conclusion does have *practical* force. For if the agent fails to carry out the action, he must, on pain of self-contradiction, reject one of the premisses. If the agent genuinely accepts that he would attain *x*, and that unless he does *y* he will not attain *x*, then he is committed to doing, or at least attempting to do, *y*, and this commitment is *logical*.

Note that optative inference requires, as a premiss, what the agent would achieve. What the reasoner would achieve is quite irrelevant, unless the reasoner is the agent. From "Uncle John would not drown," nothing follows about what James needs to do – although something may follow about what he ought to do.

Let me conclude this section with two examples of valid optative inferences:

You would have sugar in your soup.
Unless you ask the waiter, you will not have sugar in your soup.
Therefore you need to ask the waiter.

Smith would have Western win.
Unless Smith catches the pass, Western will not win.
Therefore Smith needs to catch the pass.

VI

It is now time to consider that type of practical inference which permits "should"-judgments as conclusions. For since optative inference does not lead to normative conclusions, the role of wants in optative inference sheds no light whatsoever on whether "is"-statements may entail "should"-statements.

I shall call this second type of practical inference *normative inference*. One general pattern of normative inference is:

A has reason to attain *x*.
Unless *A* does *y*, he will not attain *x*.
Therefore *A* should do *y*.

The first premiss is clearly a dummy, which is to be cashed out in particular cases by stating *A*'s reasons. But what types of statement will do this? Statements about wants? Expressions of wants? Both? Neither?

To help answer our question, consider the status of the conclusion. Let us suppose for present purposes that it may be considered to contain an imperative – and if an imperative, then surely an imperative of counsel, which is associated with that species I earlier called recommendation.

Imperatives of counsel have practical force, but not in the same manner as optatives. Imperatives of counsel are action-guiding but not action-determining. Accepting the premises of a valid optative inference commits the agent to action; accepting the premisses of a valid normative inference does not. An agent may agree with an imperative of counsel, and so agree that *reasonable* action would be determined by it, yet not actually be reasonable in his own action. One cannot settle the problem of akrasia by ruling the weak-willed man logically out of bounds.

Since the conclusion of normative inference contains an imperative, and since the premisses must entail the conclusion, then the premisses must include an imperative. But this consideration, which Hare uses to dismiss the view that one can infer "should"-statements from "is"-statements, and so from statements about wants, is also sufficient to dismiss Hare's own view that one can infer "should"-statements from expressions of wants. For as we have seen, such expressions are "would"-statements – optatives and not imperatives. The premisses of a valid normative inference must include at least one imperative, and neither an indicative nor an optative will serve.

Thus it is neither necessary nor sufficient that the agent accept the optative "I would attain x" in order to conclude that he should do y, given that y is the necesssary means to x. And equally it is neither necessary nor sufficient that the reasoner accept the optative "I would that the agent attain x" in order to conclude that the agent should do y. It is in my view true that wants provide reasons for actions, but it is clearly not the case that expressions of wants have the normative force required to entail judgments about what one should do, any more than do statements of wants.

My objection to Hare, then, is not to his insistence that practical inferences be formally valid, nor to his view that moral judgments are imperatival. Rather, accepting these, I maintain that expressions of wants, which are not imperatival, cannot entail moral judgments, or any other normative judgments.

Furthermore, let me suggest that imperativals, such as moral judgments, cannot entail actions or decisions, just because actions and decisions have an optative force lacked by imperatives. Thus Hare's view of prescriptivity is radically misconceived. Normative inference lacks prescriptive force – that is, acceptance of the conclusion does not commit one to the action – because no imperative inference can possess prescriptive force. One may always without self-contradiction accept an imperative, whether it be a command, an instruction, a recommendation, an hortation, or a request, without acting on it. Only if one accepts an optative is one logically committed to action, and acceptance of an imperative can never force one logically to acceptance of an optative.

But let us suppose now that what I have just been saying is wrong. Suppose that I am wrong to deny that optative inference is a type of imperative inference. Suppose wants are properly expressed as imperatives. It still will not follow that expressions of wants can serve as premisses in valid normative inferences, unless expressions of wants are the right sort – the right species – of imperatives to entail imperatives of *counsel*. And this I would deny. Even if "Let *A* attain *x*" appropriately expresses a want, yet it does not serve together with "Unless *A* does *y*, he will not attain *x*" to entail "*A* should do *y*."

VII

I hold that wants provide reasons for actions. We may therefore replace the first premiss of a normative inference by a statement about wants, and produce an inference which may be acceptable although not formally valid. The inference pattern is:

> *A* would attain *x*.
> Unless *B* does *y* (where *B* may or may not be the same person as *A*), *A* will not attain *x*.
> Therefore *B* should do *y*.

To accept the conclusion of such an inference is to accept

A's wants as sufficient reason for B's doing y. To reject the conclusion is to reject A's wants as sufficient reason for B's doing y. Both are permissible, and no formal rule will tell us which inferences to accept and which not, since formal inference is no longer in question.

Nothing is gained by replacing the first premiss by:

I would that A attain x (or: Let A attain x).

With this replacement, to accept the conclusion is to accept one's own want about A as sufficient reason for B's doing y, and to reject the conclusion is to reject one's own want as sufficient reason. Once again, both are permissible.

Thus there is no formal way of treating the Fischer-Botwinnik example, the Uncle John and James example, or the Tom and Jane example. In all cases, one may accept the premisses as sufficiently grounding the conclusion, or one may not, and one's logical conscience can remain clear.

VIII

I have tried to expose two pitfalls about wanting, into which I believe Hare falls. The first is that wants are correctly expressed as imperatives. The second is that expressions of wants are sufficient as premisses in logically conclusive inferences with normative conclusions. About both there is, of course, far more to be said than I can pretend to have done in what have been, I fear, very dogmatic comments.

Comments

BY D. F. PEARS

In the first section of the second part of Hare's "Wanting: Some Pitfalls" (pp. 91–92), I am supposed to have slipped into one of the pitfalls which await philosophers who deviate from the true account of intending. I do not agree with this description of my present position, and I shall try to show that it is not even precarious. I shall also do two other things in this note. I shall put Kenny's theory back where it belongs in the wider setting in which he presented it in his book *Action, Emotion and Will*,[1] and I shall say something about the larger issue which he raises there.

First, I have to deal with the so-called pitfall. Let "*A*" be the specification of a particular action. Then I would like to consider the following four sentences:

s1 I really want to do *A* (all things considered).
s2 I intend to do *A*.
s3 I will do *A*.
s4 I shall do *A*.

The part of Kenny's theory which I criticized in the lecture to which Hare refers[2] is concerned with the analysis of s2 and s3. Kenny says that, when s2 "is a genuine report of a state of mind," it "is tantamount to the statement 'I have said in my heart "Let me do *A*" ' " (p. 218). Hare protests that "this is not a very fair statement of the theory" (I repeated it in my lecture), "for it exposes it gratuitously to the objection that a man might have said in his heart 'Let me do *A*,' and then, afterwards, changed his mind and said (also in his heart) 'No, let me not do *A* after all.' Such a man would have said in his heart 'Let me do *A*,' but would not now intend to do *A*" (p. 91). I agree that Kenny ought to have added a *caveat* about change of mind, but I did not make this criticism in 1964, because it seemed to me then, as it does now, that he took the addition for granted.

1 Anthony Kenny, *Action, Emotion and Will* (London: Routledge & Kegan Paul, 1963).
2 D. F. Pears, *Predicting and Deciding*, Proceedings of the British Academy, Vol. 50 (London: Oxford University Press, 1964), pp. 193–227. Reprinted in *Studies in the Philosophy of Thought and Action*, edited by P. F. Strawson (London: Oxford University Press, 1968).

Kenny then offers an analysis of s3 and (I believe, but I am not sure of this: see p. 218, lines 11–15) of s2 when s2 is the expression of an intention. It is not clear to me how to determine when s2 is a genuine report of a state of mind and when it is the expression of an intention. So in my discussion of the analysis which he offers – which is simply "Let me do *A*" – I shall concentrate on s3 as he himself does.

Now the sentence "Let me do *A*" is (if one is not too strict about grammatical categories) in the imperative mood. In Kenny's theory is it supposed to be a command addressed to oneself? It is, I think, clear that, in order to get an answer to this question, we need examine only his analysis of s3. For, whatever force the imperative sentence has in the analysis of s3, it will also have when it is quoted in the analysis of s2 when s2 is a genuine report of a state of mind.

But, unfortunately, the question is ambiguous, at least in the context of this discussion. For Hare distinguishes two different senses of the word "command," a generic sense and a specific sense. In its generic sense it is supposed to apply to anything expressed by a sentence in the imperative mood, and in its specific sense it applies to what would ordinarily be called "a command" (see Hare, pp. 95–96). In what follows, when I use the word "command" without qualification I shall always mean "what would ordinarily be called a command." As far as I can see, Kenny too always used the word in this way in his book. Occasionally, in order to make my meaning absolutely plain, I shall insert a reminder that I am using the word in this way. On the few occasions when I use the word in what is supposed to be its other sense, I shall always say that this is what I am doing.

Let me now repeat my question. In Kenny's theory is the sentence "Let me do *A*" supposed to be a command addressed to oneself? I did not find this question of interpretation easy to answer in 1964, and I do not find it any easier now. On the one hand he says that his analysis of s3 is justified by the analogy between s3 and a command (p. 216), and this suggests that the answer to my question is negative, because the sentence "Let me do *A*" would only be like a command. But on the other hand he says, "The insincere expression of intention may be regarded as giving oneself an order in the presence of one's listener, which one does not mean oneself to obey. It is as if a superior, having received a complaint against a subordinate, should summon the subordinate and tell him in the complainer's presence 'Put this matter right,' though both superior and subordinate know that the command is not meant seriously and is issued merely to satisfy the complainer" (p. 220). This suggests an affirmative answer to my question.

Notice that this difficulty of interpretation is not produced by any doubt about the sense of the word "command." In the passage which has just been quoted Kenny uses the word "order," and in any case, as I have already pointed out, he seems always to use the word "command" in its specific sense. The difficulty is that it is not clear whether the analysis of s3 is supposed to *be*, or to *be like*, a command.

My reaction to this difficulty in 1964 was to try out both interpretations of Kenny's theory. First, in the section of my lecture to which Hare refers,[3] I criticized the theory on the assumption that s3 was supposed to be a command. Then I criticized it on the assumption that s3 was supposed only to be like a command.[4] Hare does not mention the second of these two pieces of criticism. If he had noticed it, he would have realized that I did not confuse the thesis that s3 is like a command with the thesis that it is a command (in any case, this confusion would not be the same as the confusion between the supposed generic sense of the word "command" and its specific sense, though it is true that the first of these two confusions might be produced by the second).

The reason why Hare does not notice the second of my two pieces of criticism may be that I directed it against

3 *Ibid.*, pp. 206–208.
4 *Ibid.*, pp. 208–210.

Anscombe's version of the thesis that s3 is like a command,[5] merely observing in a footnote that Kenny agreed with Anscombe that the two are alike. This was, I now see, unfair to Kenny. For it might well leave the impression that Kenny's theory has to be interpreted to mean that s3 is a command. This is far from true. For the main drift of his arguments supports the other version of his theory, and as far as I can see, there is only one passage (p. 220; already quoted) which implies that s3 is a command.

However, before I move on to the other version of the theory, which seems to me to be the more interesting of the two, I would like to make a couple of points about the version which implies that s3 is a command.

First, there is the question why, in interpreting this version of Kenny's theory, I substituted self-exhortation for self-addressed command. My reason was that there are obvious objections to taking commanding to be the speech-act which is, as it were, internalized when s3 is analyzed as "Let me do *A*." I chose self-exhortation instead, because it seemed to me to be the least inappropriate speech-act for the drama which, according to this version of the theory, would be enacted *in foro interno* every time that a person utters s3. Of course, with the other version of the theory it is not clear that there is a specific speech-act to be internalized. Certainly, there would be no need to internalize any of the speech-acts which are closely associated with the imperative mood. But I shall say more about that later, when I examine the other version of the theory.

Second, there is Hare's objection to a criticism which I directed against Kenny's analyses of s2 and s3. I think that I ought to quote rather more of my criticism than Hare does before I deal with his objection to it: "Moreover, even if the thing about which the speaker might deceive his audience when he says 'I will do *A*' or 'I intend to do *A*' had been the

5 See G. E. M. Anscombe, *Intention* (Oxford: Blackwell, 1957), pp. 55–57.

thing about which he might deceive them when he produces what the theory regards as the equivalent of these two utterances, it is also important that the method of deception suggested by the theory is too devious. For conveying information is not the primary purpose of self-exhortation, whereas it is the primary purpose of the two utterances."[6] Hare's comment on this is: "It seems to me that this lacks even the appearance of cogency as an argument against Kenny's view; for, on Kenny's view, 'I intend to do *A*' *would* have the primary purpose of informing (viz., of the fact that I subscribe to the self-addressed command to do *A*); and, on the other hand, 'I will do *A*,' which is on Kenny's view not primarily informative, is indeed not primarily informative, but rather an expression of intention or resolve" (p. 95).

Here, as at all other points in this section of his paper, Hare is defending the thesis that s3 is like a self-addressed command against a criticism directed at the thesis that s3 is a self-addressed command, or, at least, a piece of self-exhortation. For in the preceding paragraph of my lecture I had argued that a person who exhorts himself to do *A*, but who does not really mean the self-exhortation, is not deceiving his audience about his intention to do *A*, but rather about his intention to get himself to decide to do *A*; or, alternatively, if he has already decided to do *A*, but needs to keep himself up to the mark, he is deceiving his audience by pretending to reinforce his infirm intention. Therefore, I suggested, the theory makes the speaker deceive his audience about the wrong thing. I then argued, in the passage which I have just quoted, that the theory makes the speaker's method of deception too indirect. So the version of the theory which I was attacking is not the version which Hare is defending, and it might appear that no more need be said about this particular skirmish.

But there are two points in Hare's objection which I would like to take up. First, it is surely wrong to say that s3, when

6 Pears, *Predicting and Deciding*, pp. 207–208.

it is said by one person to another, is not primarily informative. In such a case its primary function is to convey two pieces of information to the hearer – that the speaker is determined to do *A*, and that he will in fact do *A*. There is of course, the problem of characterizing the way in which these two pieces of information are conveyed, and Hare's thesis, that the speaker's determination (he says "intention or resolve") is expressed, is a small contribution to half of this problem. It is also difficult to decide which of the two pieces of information is the main burden of the communication (s4 treats the first piece of information more lightly, but how much more weight does s3 put on it?). But there can surely be no doubt that the primary function of s3, when it is said by one person to another, is to convey these two pieces of information. My argument – a valid one – was simply that, if overheard self-exhortation conveys information, it conveys it indirectly and as a side-line, and therefore, s3 cannot be analyzed as a piece of self-exhortation.

The second feature of this objection of Hare's on which I would like to comment is his assumption that I did not notice that, according to Kenny, s2 "when it is a genuine report of a state of mind" (Hare omits this qualification, and I think that the omission is probably an error of interpretation), is primarily informative – it conveys the information that the speaker has said in his heart "Let me do *A*" (and has not subsequently unsaid this in his heart). In fact I had noticed this.[7] But, of course, even if the speaker of s2 did convey this piece of information, he would not thereby convey the information which is in fact conveyed by s2, unless, at the very least, the self-exhortation "Let me do *A*" itself conveyed the information conveyed by s3. Here I intended the same two criticisms to be applied again – first, the criticism (in the passage preceding Hare's quotation from my lecture) that the self-exhortation does not convey this information, and, second, the criticism (in the passage which he quotes) that

7 *Ibid.*, p. 206.

the self-exhortation does not convey any information in the direct way in which s3 conveys information. But I did not set this argument out in detail in my lecture, and I must admit that what I said could give the impression that it might depend on the false assumption that Kenny did not regard s2 as primarily informative "when it is a genuine report of a state of mind."

It is tedious to rehearse all this, particularly when the main drift of Kenny's arguments supports the other version of his theory. But perhaps it has been worth it. For, as I shall show in a moment, it is very easy to slide from the version which says that s3 is like a command to the version which says that it is a command (or a piece of self-exhortation).

I now turn to the more interesting thesis that s3 is like a command – so like a command that an imperative sentence is a suitable form of words to express an intention. According to Hare an imperative sentence is also a suitable form of words to express a desire to perform an action (p. 92). So he would say that at least the first three of my four sentences, s1–s3, could be appropriately expressed in the imperative mood, or in a form which included a quoted sentence in the imperative mood (a complication introduced by s2). He also puts wishes in the imperative camp.

Kenny gives a more detailed account of the route by which he arrives at the thesis that s3 is like a command. He believes that the auxiliary verb in s3 should be classified with other affective verbs and verbal phrases – e.g., "to intend," "to prefer," "to want," "to choose," "to desire," "to be glad," "to hope," and, negatively, "to regret," "to be ashamed," "to fear." According to him the members of this class all have something in common, something which makes it appropriate to use the language of wishes or commands in their analyses – i.e., to use the imperative mood, or one of the tenses which in English sometimes play the role of the imperative mood.

But why should anyone suppose that an imperative sentence is a suitable form of words to express what is expressed by s1 or by s3, or that a paraphrase of s2 would contain a quoted imperative sentence? And what about s4? Is it insufficiently vehement for this treatment? In his reply Gauthier complains that Hare offers little positive argument for casting imperatives in this role (p. 98). In the subsequent open discussion Hare relied on an argument which makes a brief appearance in the part of his paper which is devoted to me. "Actually, as Kenny, I think, points out, it is very plausible to say that, when Hannibal orders his troops to march on Rome, he is not merely commanding them to do so, but expressing the intention that they should do so: and this lends some plausibility to the thesis that, when I form the intention to go to Rome, I have that in my mind which would, if it were expressed in words, naturally be expressed by saying, 'Let me go to Rome,' or, if I were to address myself in military style in the mood which I was taught in the army to call the future imperative, 'Hare will go to Rome,' or 'I will go to Rome' " (p. 94).

This is a very weak argument. If the verb "to express" is used, as Hare uses it here, to signify a loose bond, there are all sorts of locutions which might express the intention that another, or others should do *A*. Why pick on imperative sentences for this role? Why, as Davidson asked in the discussion, assume that there is any single locution (other than "I intend that you should do *A*") to which this role ought to be assigned on the ground that it is generally and pre-eminently suited to it? Of course, in the particular case chosen by Hare, Hannibal's position makes it especially appropriate for him to use an imperative sentence. For he is in a position to secure the achievement of his intention by issuing a command (specific sense) to his troops. But this is not true in general of people who have such intentions.

Even if it were generally true that a person who intended that another should do something was in a position to issue a command (specific sense), or to use the imperative mood in one of the milder speech-acts that are closely associated with it, that would not support Hare's thesis. For, as he insists in his paper, his thesis is not that intentions are (or find expression in) internalized commands (specific sense). Nor, as far as I can see, does he think that any of the other speech-acts which are closely associated with the imperative mood would be a better candidate for internalization (see Gauthier's "Comments," p. 103). His point is, rather, that what is internalized is the essence of the imperative mood when it has been extracted from the different speech-acts which are closely associated with it.

But, though this is his point, it is, I think, significant that in the passage just quoted he flirts with the other version of the theory, which I dealt with in the first part of this note: "... or, if I were to address myself in military style in the mood which I was taught in the army to call the future imperative, 'Hare will go to Rome,' or 'I will go to Rome.' " This suggests that, when Hare substitutes "I" for "Hare," a command (specific sense) is internalized. Naturally, he would not endorse this suggestion, but its presence is revealing. It fills an uncomfortable vacuum, and makes us feel that we understand what is supposed to be going on when Hare says "Let me go to Rome." But, since, according to Hare's and Kenny's preferred version of the theory, the internalization of this locution does not carry with it the internalization of any of the speech-acts which are closely associated with the imperative mood, I doubt if we do understand what is supposed to be going on.

It is merely an expository device to skate as close as possible to the other version of the theory, but it can be taken too far. On one occasion, as I have already shown, Kenny actually slides into a defence of the other version. In *The Language of Morals* Hare is more circumspect. In Chapter II he introduces the concepts of affirming and assenting to a command (generic sense). In cases which involve two people, to affirm is to address it to the other person, and, at the receiving end, to assent to it is to agree to carry it out. But, when a person addresses a command (generic sense) to himself, Hare says that "affirmation and assent are identical. It is logically impossible for a man to dissent from what he himself is affirming (though of course he may not be sincere in affirming it)."[8] Here, too, if we allow our minds to slide over to the other version of the theory, as is only too easy, we shall feel that we understand what is supposed to be going on. For the other version would allow some distinction *in foro interno* between the issuing end of a first person command (generic sense) and the receiving end, and the thesis would be that it is logically necessary that sincere affirmation of such a command should be accompanied by sincere assent to it (i.e., by sincere agreement to carry it out). No doubt, this thesis is vulnerable to objections, but it is intelligible, and it owes its intelligibility to the idea that one of the speech-acts which are closely associated with the imperative mood is internalized. But if there is no distinction *in foro interno* between the issuing and receiving ends of a first person command (generic sense), and if there is no internalized speech-act closely associated with the imperative mood, what is supposed to be going on?

This question is not unanswerable. The answer to it is simply that Hare is expressing his intention to himself. So we must not put any emphasis on the fact that Hannibal was issuing a command (specific sense) to his troops. All our emphasis must be on the fact that he was expressing his intention. But if we take this line, we must abandon the thesis that an imperative sentence is a generally and pre-eminently suitable form of words to express an intention. For the bond between an intention and an imperative sentence is loose and one-many [it just happened that Hannibal was in a position to express (loose sense of this word) his intention by commanding (specific sense) his troops to march on Rome]. Moreover this particular case does not even support the less ambitious thesis that an imperative sentence is *a* suitable form of words to express an intention. For the thing

8 *The Language of Morals* (Oxford: The Clarendon Press, 1952), p. 20.

which made it appropriate for Hannibal to express (loose sense) his intention by issuing a command (generic sense) was precisely that he was in a position to issue a command (specific sense). But the appropriateness of a command (specific sense) absolutely depended on the fact that what he was expressing (loose sense) was his intention *that they should march on Rome*. So how does this case lend any plausibility to the thesis that an imperative sentence is a suitable form of words to express the speaker's intention *to do something himself*? When this version of the theory is argued for in this way, it is not surprising that we get an uncomfortable feeling which vanishes only when we add a rider which is no part of the theory – the rider that one of the speech-acts which is closely associated with the imperative mood (unlike expressing an intention) is internalized.

But there is an argument which, if it were valid, would provide appropriate support for the thesis that an imperative sentence is a suitable form of words (but not preeminently suitable) to express an intention. Hare alludes to the argument, and Kenny actually gives it. The argument is that, if we extract the essence of the imperative mood from the different speech-acts which are closely associated with it [not loosely associated with it, like "expressing" in the sentence "Hannibal's command (specific sense) expressed his intention that his army should march on Rome"], we shall find that this same essence is shared by s1, s2, and s3 (but not, apparently, by s4). In fact, according to Kenny, the same essence is shared by all the affective words and verbal phrases which would be included in a complete list governed by a principle of selection which is sufficiently determined by his examples ("to intend," "to prefer," "to want," etc.). Now it would help us in logic if a single form of words were chosen to express the essential feature of all these different locutions.[9] So *we might as well choose* the imperative mood for this role.

This argument cuts a path through the jungle of English

9 Hare's paper, p. 89; Kenny, *Action, Emotion and Will*, pp. 213–215.

usage (Hare, Hannibal, and the British Army), and goes straight to the heart of the matter. But what is the heart of the matter? What is the essential feature of all these different locutions? The surprising thing is that, though Hare shows a strong feeling for the genus, he does not tell us what he supposes the generic property to be. It is the great merit of Kenny's treatment of this subject that he does tell us what he supposes the generic property to be.

At this point in my 1964 lecture I switched attention from Kenny's account of what is common to these different locutions to Anscombe's account of what is common to intentions and commands (specific sense here and hereafter). I had two reasons for doing this. First, the central point in Kenny's more far-reaching theory is the analogy between intentions and commands, and, second, Anscombe's account of this analogy, which Kenny largely adopts and develops over a wider field, contains a more detailed list of the supposed points of similarity. However, as I have already confessed, when I switched attention to Anscombe's account of this analogy, I gave the impression that Kenny confined himself to the thesis that s2 and s3 actually are commands (or pieces of self-exhortation), and that he did not develop the thesis that they are like commands. But in fact he spent most of his time developing the thesis that they are like commands, and I shall now concentrate on what he says in support of that thesis, quoting Anscombe's views only when Kenny quotes them.

The thesis that there is an analogy between s3 (or any of my other three sentences) and a command is of little interest unless the point of analogy is specified. Kenny's first specification of what he regards as the central point of analogy is the following:

There is, in fact, an important logical feature common to commands [sc., specific sense], wishes, and expressions of intention, which distinguishes them from statements. If a man sincerely utters a statement which fails to accord with the facts, then he is mistaken; if he utters a command, a wish, or an expression of intention, then he is not mistaken merely because the facts do not accord with his utterances (p. 216).

The footnote which Kenny attaches to his text at this point contains the following long quotation from Anscombe's book *Intention*:

There is a difference between the types of ground on which we call an order and an estimate of the future sound. The reasons justifying an order are not ones suggesting what is probable or likely to happen, but, e.g., ones suggesting what it would be good to make happen with a view to an objective, or with a view to a sound objective. In this regard, commands and expressions of intention are similar ...

Let us consider a man going round a town with a shopping list in his hand. Now it is clear that the relation of this list to the things he actually buys is one and the same whether his wife gave him the list or it is his own list; and that there is a different relation when a list is made by a detective following him about. If he made the list himself, it was an expression of intention; if his wife gave it to him, it has the role of an order. What then is the identical relation to what happens, in the order and the intention, which is not shared by the record? It is precisely this: if the list and the things that the man actually buys do not agree, and if this and this alone constitutes a *mistake*, then the mistake is not in the list but in the man's performance; whereas if the detective's record and what the man actually buys do not agree, then the mistake is in the record.[10]

Kenny then endorses this last point of Anscombe's, and goes on to disagree with something else that she says, viz., "that there is no reason other than a dispensable usage why we should not call commands true and false according as they were obeyed and disobeyed."

10 Anscombe, *Intention*, pp. 55–56.

E

Since I have now moved outside the area of the discussion at the Colloquium, my comments on this text will be sketchy, although it is of central importance.

Consider, first, the question whether the suggested analogy holds between a command and s4. Of course, the claim that it does not would not be a direct criticism of this version of Kenny's theory. For, as far as I can see, if we asked which of my four sentences are, according to him, expressions of intention, his answer would be s3 and s2, when s2 is not a genuine report of a state of mind, but not s4. But a theory which claims to isolate the essential feature of the genus to which intentions belong surely ought to apply to s4. So, if the suggested analogy does not hold between a command and s4, that would be a damaging limitation.

Now anyone who utters s4 to someone else, whatever else he does, conveys two pieces of information, the information that he intends to do A, and the information that he will in fact do A. It is true that the exact analysis of s4 is a difficult matter. But, fortunately, it is not necessary for me to try to determine which of the two pieces of information is the main burden of the communication, e.g., whether both facts are asserted, or one is in some way implied, etc. The only point that I need to make here is that the second piece of information is not cancellable – e.g., the speaker of s4 could not cancel it by continuing, "... but, in fact, A is impossible." He could not even mitigate it by reducing the categorical force of this part of his communication, e.g., by the continuation, "... but, as a matter of fact, I probably shall not be able to do A." So it seems to me that, whenever someone utters s4, it will not be correct unless it fits his future performance.

If the Anscombe-Kenny argument were applied to s4 (and, as I said, Kenny does not apply it to s4), it might appear to undermine this conclusion. For s4 expresses (in some sense) an intention, and, if the speaker fails to carry out his intention (through inefficiency, let us suppose), the mistake would appear to be in his performance (assuming that he has not changed his mind in the meantime). But this is a very weak argument. It depends on a tendentious use of the phrase "the mistake." Why must we assume that, in the circumstances described, the speaker has made only one mistake, a mistake in his performance? It is surely obvious that he has made two mistakes, one in his performance (which failed to fit his intention), and one in his earlier utterance (which failed to fit his performance).

I made this criticism of the suggested analogy between intentions and commands in *Predicting and Deciding* (p. 209). As far as s4 is concerned (and Kenny does not bring s4 into the discussion), it seems to me to be a sufficient criticism. It is true that it does not take any notice of a third type of mistake which is mentioned by Anscombe in the passage quoted by Kenny (and taken up by Kenny in a later passage in his book, which I shall quote at the end of this note), the mistake made by an agent who intentionally acts wrongly (in some sense of this vague adverb), or (derivatively) the mistake made by an agent who forms a wrong intention, or by someone else who commands him to act wrongly. But I think that it is obvious that the possibility of this kind of mistake has no effect whatsoever on the *general* question whether s4 ought to fit the agent's future action, or his future action ought to fit the intention which in some loose sense s4, whatever else it does, expresses, or both.

Now let us look at s3 in order to see whether there is a better case for maintaining, as Anscombe and Kenny actually do maintain, that the suggested analogy holds between s3 and a command. It seems to me that the case for the analogy between these two is no better than the case for the analogy between s4 and a command. It is true that s3 expresses a greater degree of determination than s4, but this is entirely compatible with its conveying the second of the two pieces of information – viz., that the speaker will in fact do *A*. And it does convey this piece of information. For the cancellation and the mitigation, which were found to be impossible for s4 are also impossible for s3.

I think it probable that the reason why supporters of the version of the theory which I am now criticizing usually concentrate on s3 to the neglect of s4 is that the use of s3 suggests that there may have been, or may be, quite a lot of warming up of the engine before the agent actually moves off; and this may seem to require a self-addressed command, or at least a piece of self-exhortation. But I hope that I have shown that this version of the theory cannot get any support from that quarter.

However, the fact that s3 is used to express a special degree of determination does suggest an interesting question: if we take the facts conveyed by s3, and subtract from them the fact that the speaker will actually do A, what is left? Note that this question is not the same as the question, what is left when someone utters s3 and then cancels part of it by continuing: "... but in fact A is impossible." For, as I said just now, s3 cannot be cancelled in this way, and the question which I am now asking does not imply that it can be. An obvious answer to my question is that what is left is the fact conveyed by s1, or perhaps the fact conveyed by s1 when s1 is followed, as it certainly can be followed, by the continuation: "... but in fact A is impossible." But is this fact the whole of what is left? Or, if we want the whole of what is left, ought we to add a little more, and say that the total residue is the fact conveyed by s2, or perhaps the fact conveyed by s2, when s2 is followed by that continuation? But I do not think that we can go quite as far as this, because the intention to do A is not compatible with the belief that A is impossible. Nor does the determination to do A seem to be compatible with this belief ("to try to do A" would be better). However, s2, at least, can be followed by the continuation which mitigates its force: "... but, as a matter of fact, I probably shall not be able to do A."

But these are tentative suggestions about complex questions of analysis. If they are mistaken, that will not undermine my simple criticism of the thesis that the suggested analogy holds between s3 and a command. As I have already pointed out, Kenny's analysis of s2, when it is a genuine report of a state of mind, contains his analysis of s3, and, since this does not convey the information which is, in fact, conveyed by s3, his analysis of s2 must be incorrect.

There are three final points that I would like to make.

First, I do not claim to have dealt with all Anscombe's further developments of the basic idea which I have been criticizing.[11]

Second, it is only fair to Kenny to point out that, when he is explaining what he supposes all the various items on his list to have in common, he often gives pride of place to wishes alongside intentions – e.g., he does this in the first sentence of my last quotation from his book. I am not sure how important this is. Perhaps the explanation is that in his list the verb "to wish" is the only one which sometimes signifies a speech-act which is closely associated with the imperative mood (or with something which might be classified as the imperative mood); and that the verb "to wish" is substitutable for the verb "to want" in s1 without change of sense. This might make it look as if this verb could be used as the central span of a bridge connecting s1 directly with a speech-act closely associated with the imperative mood, and so indirectly connecting all the affective verbs and verbal phrases on Kenny's list with the whole family of speech-acts which are closely associated with the imperative mood. But, as Kenny points out (pp. 215–216), a wish (expressed in the imperative mood, or in something like it) is appropriate only when what is wished for is not that the wisher himself should perform some action (cf., my point about Hannibal's intention and the imperative mood). In any case the version of the theory which I am now criticizing does not require the construction of this kind of bridge between usages even if it

11 See *Intention, passim.*

could be satisfactorily completed. For this version says only
that *we might as well use* the imperative mood to analyze
sentences containing verbs on Kenny's list, because they all
belong to the same genus as commands.

Finally, I would like to emphasize that the thesis that an
intention is like a command is only a small part of this version
of Kenny's theory, and so my criticism of the theory has been
developed on a narrow front – e.g., I have not argued that
wishes expressed in the imperative mood are unlike commands. My point has been that the particular analogy which
Kenny sees between a command and s3 does not exist, and
that this analogy does not hold between a command and s4
either (and he does not claim that it does hold here). About
his analysis of s2, when s2 is a genuine report of a state of
mind, I have said little more than that it contains his analysis
of s3, with which it fails. These arguments of mine are more
restricted in scope than his total theory. I shall end this note
with a final quotation from his book which will show how
much more restricted in scope my arguments are:

Despite, therefore, the varied constructions which follow
affective verbs, it seems that the one distinction of logical
importance is between two modes of speech which we may call
the indicative and the optative. In the first mode, the facts, or
what happens, sets the standard by which the utterance is
judged and found true or false; in the second mode, the
utterance sets the standard by which the facts, or what happens,
is judged and found good or bad. *Verum et falsum in mente,
bonum et malum in rebus.* That is to say, whether a statement or
a belief is true or false depends on what the facts are; the facts
are the standard by which statements and beliefs are judged.
On the other hand, whether an agent makes a mistake in what he
does depends on what his intentions are; whether a subject's
actions are obedient or disobedient depends on what his
master's commands were; whether a citizen acts legally or
illegally depends on what the laws are; whether a particular

state of affairs is good or bad depends on what somebody wants. In all these cases, a Volition[12] is the standard by which what happens is judged (pp. 220–221).

I do not share this view of the great watershed dividing the two modes of speech. Perhaps the terrain looks like this when it is viewed from a great height, and perhaps it is a good thing to begin by trying to draw this line right across the map. But, if we try to relate intentions to this line, the most plausible thing that we can say is that it cuts through them, and splits the sentences which express them into two elements, one concerned with the speaker's future performance, the other concerned with the speaker at the moment. But then it is at least an oversimplification to characterize the second of these two elements as "the imperative (or optative) element." For its characterization is a much more complex matter than the use of these grammatical terms suggests.

12 "Volition" is his name for what is common to all the items on his list (pp. 214–215). So in this passage he calls the mode of speech to which they all belong "the optative mode." His thesis is that we might as well use the imperative mood to express what is common to them all.

4 / Two Problems about Reasons for Actions

D. F. Pears

To give my reason for my action is to connect it with my desires and factual beliefs. I need not always describe both, because sometimes the description of my operative desires makes it obvious what my factual beliefs must have been, and *vice versa*. Nor need I always describe my action when I give my reason for it. But my statement of my reason will always rest on three descriptions, explicit or implicit in what I say, a description of my action, a description of my operative desires, and a description of my relevant factual beliefs.

This is a rough account of what it is for an agent to give his reason for his action. It uses the words "desire" and "belief" in very unrestricted ways: it does not mention the idiosyncrasies of evaluative statements, and it contains other oversimplifications. But it is sufficiently accurate to serve as a basis for the introduction of my two problems, which are about the available descriptions of desires and actions. Is it possible to take any agent's reason for his action, and to find a description of his operative desire under which, given his factual beliefs, it contingently produced his action? And is it possible to find a description of his action under which it contingently issued from his operative desire?[1]

---

1 (Added after the discussion). When my two questions are formulated in this way, they are open to the following interpretation: "Is it

It may appear that I have not got two problems here, but only one. But an example will show that there really are two. Suppose that someone shoots a rabbit, and, asked why, says that he shot it because he just felt like shooting it. Then it may be hard to see how his desire, described in this way, given certain background conditions, one of which would be his factual beliefs, could conceivably have failed to produce his action, as originally described. It may also be hard to see how his action, as originally described, given that it was intentional, could conceivably have issued from any other desire than the one described. These are clearly two distinct

possible to take any agent's reason for his action, and to find a description which applies to his operative desire, and which does not make it an *a priori* statement that that desire, under that description, given his factual beliefs, produced his action? ... etc." The formulation of the two question which I use at the end of the next paragraph is also open to this interpretation. On this interpretation my two problems would be problems about the identification of desires and actions (about the available ways of making identifying references to them), and the solutions to them would be easy – e.g., any *a priori* connection could be severed by describing the desire as the desire which the agent first felt at a specified moment.

But I did not intend these two formulations of my two questions to be taken in this way, and I overlooked the possibility that they might be taken in this way. I intended them to be taken in the following way: "Is it possible to take any agent's reason for his action, and to find a description which applies to his operative desire, and which makes it contingently true that that desire, under that description, given his factual beliefs, produced his action? ... etc.": and I supposed that, in order that this should be contingently true, it would not be enough that the description should apply to the desire and that the desire should have produced the action, but that it would also be necessary that there should be some general connection between the desire, under that description, and the action. That is, I intended the two preliminary formulations of my questions to be taken in the way in which they are presented in the fifth and subsequent paragraphs of this paper.

If it appears that I was concerned with the more general question, whether there are any descriptions of desires and actions under which they do not have *a priori* connections with one another, that is because my phraseology in the first four paragraphs of this paper is, I regret, ambiguous. The reasons (good or bad) for maintaining that the Humean requirement can (or cannot) be met in this area are more specific than the considerations which are relevant to the more general inquiry into the descriptions available for making identifying references to desires and actions without producing *a priori* connections between them.

difficulties. First, the desire is taken as a sufficient condition of the action which was to be explained, and the question is whether its sufficiency can be presented as contingent sufficiency. Second, it is taken as a necessary condition, and the same question is asked about its necessity.

These two questions may seem to be not very difficult to answer. For it may appear that, if the desire, taken as a sufficient condition of the action, has an *a priori* connection with it, that is only because the desire and the action are presented under descriptions which happen to match one another. It just happens that the action is described as shooting the rabbit, and that the desire is described as the desire to shoot the rabbit. But even if the agent has to use that description of his desire, because that was his reason, he might still apply a non-matching description to his action. For there are many different ways of shooting a particular rabbit, so that even with that description of his desire it is an open contingency which way it was shot. And the question about the desire taken as a necessary condition of his action may seem even easier to answer. For even if the agent has to use that description of his desire, it is only a contingent fact that he has to use it. He might have shot the rabbit because he wanted to eat it. So it may be said that the original description of the action, "shooting the rabbit," leaves it an open contingency from what desire it issued.

I do not think that these answers solve my two problems. But before I take them up, I wish to put the problems themselves in a wider setting. They are usually posed in the course of a discussion of the question whether agents' reasons for actions are causes. But this is really too narrow a setting for them. For they are produced by the general requirement that *explicanda* and *explicantia* should have descriptions under which they are universally and contingently connected with one another, and it is as natural to make this generalized Humean requirement when an explanatory connection is not causal as it is when it is causal. Moreover, there are special

features of the concept of cause which introduce complica-
tions which are irrelevant to the two problems. So here they
will be posed in the setting of the general Humean requirement which produces them. If that requirement could be
abandoned, the two problems would vanish: they would be
solved if descriptions of desires and actions which satisfied it
could be found.

So one possible procedure would be to examine the
Humean requirement, that *explicanda* and *explicantia* should
have descriptions under which they are universally, or at least
generally, and contingently connected with one another in
order to see if it can be abandoned. In fact, I shall raise the
question whether it can be abandoned when a desire is
offered as a necessary condition of an action. But I shall not
go into the question whether it can be abandoned when a
desire is offered as a sufficient condition of an action. For in
the latter case it seems to be peculiarly difficult to abandon
the requirement, because there are occasions when the
agent's knowledge, that he will do a particular thing in the
future, is based on his present desires. No doubt, there are
also occasions when he just knows that he will do it. But the
existence of the other sort of occasion, when his knowledge
does have a present basis, makes it peculiarly difficult to
abandon the Humean requirement at this point. It seems
that in such cases there must be something in the agent's
present psychological state which is connected with his
future behaviour generally and contingently. If the connection were not general, his claim that he would perform the
action would not be reliable, and, if the connection were
not contingent, his claim would not have a present basis.
Here I am not arguing that such claims are reliable only when
they have a present basis. My argument requires only the
premiss that, as a matter of contingent fact, they sometimes
do have a present basis. A different, and more ambitious
argument would be that, even when they do not have what
would usually be regarded as a present basis, the agent's

spontaneous inclination to make the claim could be regarded as a present basis. But I shall rely on the less ambitious argument.

I shall strengthen this argument later. If it can be made cogent, then at least when desires are taken as sufficient conditions of actions, they ought to have descriptions under which they are generally and contingently connected with them. That is why, instead of questioning the validity of the Humean requirement at this point, I shall look for descriptions of desires and actions which satisfy it. If the argument which I have just given can be made cogent, the case for proceeding in this way will be a strong one. For if the agent's claim, that he will do a particular thing in the future, does sometimes have a basis in his present psychological state, then we ought to be able to describe his state in a way that satisfies the Humean requirement. If we cannot produce such a description of it, that will be because we lack ingenuity rather than because we need to make some further discovery about desires (e.g., some further discovery about their neurology). So when a desire is taken as a sufficient condition of an action, it ought to be possible to demonstrate that the Humean requirement is satisfied by actually producing the required description. When a desire is taken as a necessary condition of an action, it may be impossible to defend the Humean requirement by demonstrating that it is satisfied. It may also be impossible to defend it in this way in other areas, when desires and actions are not involved. But if I am right, then, when a desire is taken as a sufficient condition of an action, the situation is the reverse of what it is usually supposed to be. The situation is not that it seems necessary to press the Humean requirement at this point only because it is generally plausible: rather, it is peculiarly difficult to abandon it at this point, even for someone who is prepared to abandon it elsewhere.

Let me now resume the discussion of the two questions. I shall begin with the second one – whether an action can be given a description under which it is contingently connected with whatever desire is offered as its necessary condition – because that is the simpler question of the two. First, it is worth observing that, when an agent states his reason he does not always either state or imply that a certain desire was a necessary condition of his action. The clearest way of saying this would be to say, for example, "I would not have shot the rabbit unless I had just felt like shooting it." So let us suppose that the agent makes this statement. Then the original difficulty was that his description of his action seems to imply that his desire, as described by him, was a logically necessary condition of it. But the suggestion was that this difficulty vanishes when we reflect that it is only a contingent fact that he shot the rabbit for that reason, which is, incidentally, the limiting case of a reason for an action: he might have shot it because he wanted to eat it. However I claimed that this suggestion does not solve the problem, and I shall now try to substantiate this claim.

It is true that, if the agent, when asked for his reason, says, "I would not have shot it unless I had just felt like shooting it," this does exclude other possible reasons. For it implies that his desire to shoot it did not consist of one or more component desires describable in other ways – for instance, that it did not have as its single component the desire to eat the rabbit, and that it did not consist of two components, the desire to eat it and the desire to protect his vegetables, etc. However, this merely shifts my problem to another place. For whatever the composition of his desire to shoot it, *if he shot it intentionally*, his shooting it must have issued from that desire. So though the agent's statement of his reason does not run foul of the Humean requirement, something else does seem to run foul of it, namely the statement that his desire to shoot it, whatever its composition, was a necessary condition of his shooting it. This statement is not contingent as it stands, and it is difficult to see what alternative description of the action would turn it into a contingent statement.

But it might be objected that even in this form the problem is illusory. For the statement, that his desire to shoot it was a necessary condition of his shooting it, would more naturally be taken to exclude a certain class of other possible reasons. For it implies that his desire to shoot it was wholly spontaneous – certainly that neither it nor any of its components was the result of coercion, and possibly that neither it nor any of its components was the result of obligation. However, as I said at the beginning, I am using the word "desire" in an inclusive way so that it covers desires which are not wholly spontaneous. When the word is used in this way, the statement means that his shooting the rabbit was an action under that description. The only two possibilities that it excludes, given that the event occurred – his shooting the rabbit – are, first, that it was an unintentional action under that description, and, second, that it was a mere bodily movement. It excludes these two possibilities by giving the earlier necessary condition of the event. But the trouble is that the description of the event would itself be taken to apply to it as an intentional action (unless this implication is explicitly cancelled), and, when it is taken in this way, the rest of the statement – the part which gives the necessary condition – is not contingent, and so the problem still remains. Either the Humean requirement must be abandoned, or a description of the action which satisfies it must be found. A description of the action which satisfied it would be one under which the desire was its contingently necessary condition – or, to put the same thing the other way round, one under which it was the contingently sufficient condition of the desire.

However, this dilemma might appear to be insufficiently subtle. For it might be suggested that, although the statement, that the desire to perform action A is a necessary condition of performing action A, may satisfy the Humean requirement, because there may be descriptions of A under which that desire is its contingently necessary condition, nevertheless such descriptions are restricted in an important way. They would have to be physical descriptions of A, because the only relevant psychological description of it would be one which specified the desire from which it issued, and that description would not satisfy the Humean requirement. But a physical description of A would be a description of A as a bodily movement and not a description of it as the action A. Therefore, there is no description of A as the action A which satisfies the Humean requirement.

But this argument depends on an equivocal use of the phrase "description of A as a bodily movement." The conclusion, that there is no description of A as the action A which satisfies the Humean requirement, would follow only if the phrase meant either "description which applies to A only if it is a mere bodily movement" or "description which applies to A whether it is the action A or a mere bodily movement." The conclusion would not follow if the phrase simply meant "description of A by its physical characteristics." For a description of A by its physical characteristics might apply only if it were the action A. Such a description would be a description of it as the action A, in the relevant sense of the phrase, and it would meet the Humean requirement. Perhaps we ought to stipulate that the description must be a description of A by its intrinsic physical characteristics, in order to exclude descriptions which bring in antecedent brain states, because descriptions which did that might be thought to bring in desires, and so might be thought to fail to satisfy the Humean requirement. Now the argument gives no reason whatsoever for supposing that there is no such description of those bodily movements which are actions waiting to be discovered. Certainly, no such description has yet been discovered, and so the validity of the Humean requirement has not been directly vindicated at this point. But the attempt to prove that it could not be vindicated at this point is unsuccessful.

It is, however, an understatement to say that nobody has yet discovered a description of an action which satisfies the

Humean requirement when the desire to perform the action
is taken as its necessary condition. It is true that no such
description has yet been discovered. But it is also true that,
if anyone claims that it is there waiting to be discovered, he
cannot support this claim by pointing to some feature of our
actual use of the concepts of "desire" and "action." In the
other case, where the desire is taken as the sufficient condition
of the action, given certain background conditions, the
parallel claim can be supported in this way. For the agent's
knowledge that he will do a particular thing is often based on
his present psychological state. But when the desire is taken
as a necessary condition of the action, it is not possible to
argue in this way for the satisfiability of the Humean requirement. For in everyday life we simply do not possess the
general ability to distinguish between those bodily movements which are actions and those which are mere bodily
movements without using as a criterion the presence or
absence of the relevant desire. So there is not this reason for
supposing that those bodily movements which are actions
have an intrinsic characteristic which distinguishes them
from the others, and which we ought to be able to specify if
we were sufficiently ingenious. It is true that there are various
intrinsic characteristics of bodily movements which do give
some indication of their classification. For example, a very
complicated movement was probably produced by a desire.
But this indication is far from being as certain as the agent's
sincere report of his desire, and the simplicity of a movement
does not even make it probable that it was not produced by
a desire. Nor is it relevant to point out that the agent himself
is not surprised by those movements of his which were
produced by his own desires. For he is not surprised by
them only because he knows their origin. So it seems that we
simply do not have the material for constructing an intrinsic
criterion as reliable as the criterion which is based on the
agent's desire. If we had the general ability to distinguish
between the two classes of bodily movements without relying

on the presence or absence of the relevant desire, it could be argued that we must be using – perhaps in an extended sense of this verb – material out of which we could construct a description which would satisfy the Humean requirement. But we do not have this general ability.

If the Humean requirement cannot be vindicated in this case, perhaps its scope ought to be restricted, and it ought not to be applied to this case. Now it would be very artificial merely to treat as an exception the case in which the desire to do A is taken as a necessary condition of doing A. But there is a more general restriction of the Humean requirement which might be defended, and which would produce the effect that this case would fall among the exceptions. It might be argued that the Humean requirement applies only to sufficient conditions which precede what they produce, and not to sufficient conditions which are subsequent to what they indicate. For suppose that we take a class of events, K, and observe that many events in this class are followed by the result R_1 and that many other events in the class are followed by the result R_2 and that all events in the class are followed either by R_1 or by R_2. Then we might use this difference in the sequel as a criterion for dividing the original class, K, into two subclasses, K_1 and K_2. But if someone suggested that the only difference between the two subclasses was that members of K_1 are followed by members of R_1, whereas members of K_2 are followed by members of R_2, most people would protest that there must be some intrinsic characteristics of K_1 and K_2, waiting to be discovered, each of which would be contingently connected with one of the two sequels. If, however, we change this case merely by reversing the time-order, the parallel suggestion would not meet with such a general parallel protest. For most people would be prepared to accept the following description of the situation: There is a class of events, B (bodily movements which have a specific character and/or produce a specific result): all events in class B are preceded either by D (the relevant desire) or by N (whatever neural state produces the mere bodily movement B): so we use this difference in antecedents[2] as a criterion for distinguishing two subclasses within B, B_1 (the actions) and B_2 (the mere bodily movements): it is logically necessary that a member of B_1 should have been preceded by D, and that a member of B_2 should have been preceded by N, and there is no further difference between B_1 and B_2 waiting to be discovered.

What, if anything, is wrong with this description of the situation? If we add that D is a sufficient condition of B given the background conditions, and that N is a sufficient condition of B (which is implicit in the description given), we simply have a case of plurality of earlier sufficient conditions of B, in which the disjunction of the sufficient conditions is a necessary condition of B. In such a case we might well divide the class B according to the difference in origin, and few would protest that there must be some further difference between the two subclasses B_1 and B_2. But there would certainly be a general protest at the parallel treatment of the other situation in which the class K, which is subdivided in this way, is a class of events which are the earlier sufficient conditions of what they produce. In order to achieve exact parallelism between the two situations (except, of course, for time-order), we may add that R_1 is a later sufficient condition of K_1, and that R_2 is a later sufficient condition of K_2. But that would not affect the protest, that there must be something about K_1 in virtue of which it produces R_1, and something about K_2 in virtue of which it produces R_2.

However natural this discrimination between the two situations may be, is it justified? Are there really general grounds for not applying the Humean requirement to the case in which the desire to do A is taken as a necessary condition of doing A? Having raised this question, I shall not

---

2 The third possibility, that the event is an unintentional action, is here omitted, because it introduces a complication which is irrelevant at this point.

pursue it. I shall not pursue it, because I am more concerned with the way in which we actually use the concepts of desire and action than with the general scope of the Humean requirement. Theory apart, we use the concepts in a way that makes the statement, that the desire to do A is a necessary condition of doing A, analytic, or at least criterially true, and there is nothing in our practice which suggests that with sufficient ingenuity we ought now to be able to produce a description of A which would transform this statement into a contingent statement. Even if such a description is theoretically requisite, we do not feel that we need it in order to explain our practice. We classify some bodily movements as actions solely by virtue of their origins. This practice makes the statement, that the agent did A only because he had the desire to do A, partly tautological, provided that the word "desire" is used as I have been using it – i.e., both inclusively, and without prejudice to the possible analysis of the desire into components. But this does not indicate any peculiarity in the connection between desire and action. For there are many similar cases in which we divide a class into two subclasses using as a criterion a difference in origin, without there being any reason to suppose that we are also using (in an extended sense of that verb) some intrinsic difference between the two subclasses. What would indicate a peculiarity in the connection between desire and action would be a proof that the Humean requirement cannot be satisfied in this case, and must be satisfied in all such cases. But neither of these two points has been established.

My second problem is concerned with desires taken as sufficient conditions of actions. The question is whether desires have descriptions under which they are generally and contingently connected with the actions which they produce. This question has received more discussion than the parallel question about actions, when the desires which produced them are taken as their necessary conditions, partly because it is the more difficult of the two questions, and partly because it seems to offer a better chance of refuting the thesis that desires cause actions. But this question too ought to be posed in the wider setting of the generalized Humean requirement without regard to the special features of the concept of cause.

I assume that the Humean requirement should not be abandoned at this point, and, since my defence of this assumption has been brief, I shall amplify it later. Can some description of desires which will meet the requirement be found? It is most obviously difficult to find such a description when we take a case in which the description of the desire matches the description of the action: "I shot the rabbit just because I felt like shooting it." This statement normally means that that desire was the sufficient condition of the action given certain background conditions, whether it was also its necessary condition or not. But the difficulty is that in this sort of case, when the desire and the action are given matching descriptions, the desire is presented as the logically sufficient condition of the action, given the background conditions.

It is important to distinguish this difficulty, which is a real one, from another totally illusory difficulty, with which it is sometimes confused. A desire consists, roughly, of two elements, an object and an attitude of a certain strength towards the object. No difficulty is produced by the fact that a desire is, and for some purposes must be, described through its object. For when an attitude is described through its object, the actual realization of the object is not always a logically necessary condition of the existence of the attitude. For example, fear of stammering may contingently produce stammering, because this result is not a logically necessary condition of the existence of the attitude. So it is an illusion to suppose that it is the description of the desire through its object, the action, which makes it difficult to present the connection between the two as a contingent connection. What makes this difficult is the other element which is, and, in order to achieve an adequate explanation, must be mentioned in the description of the desire – the type and strength of the attitude.

This difficulty is not resolved by the observation which was made earlier, that there are, for instance, many different ways of shooting a particular rabbit. For all the various possible successful bodily movements must be collected under a description under which the desire to shoot the rabbit is their sufficient condition (given the background conditions). The requisite description cannot be the sort of description which was given earlier – "Bodily movement which results in the shooting of the rabbit" – because at this point we need to exclude successful but accidental shooting of the rabbit. We also need to include genuine but unsuccessful attempts to shoot it. For we wish to describe the result as specifically as we can without thereby making the generalized claim, that such desires are the sufficient conditions of such actions, false. Both the exclusion and the inclusion would be achieved by the description: "Bodily movement which is believed by the agent at the time to be going to result, or at least to have some chance of resulting in the shooting of the rabbit." But it is important to remember that, when we use this description, we have to add a stipulation about the way in which the desire produces the bodily movement, proleptically describable as the "action." For the agent might make a movement which caused the gun to go off and resulted in the shooting of the rabbit, and he might believe at the time that it was going to have this result, and yet the movement might only be a gesture of impatience produced by his desire to shoot the rabbit. So we have to stipulate (as, in fact, I have already done, but rather inconspicuously) that the movement be produced not by the desire alone, but by the desire together with the agent's relevant factual belief. Then we can use the suggested description without including cases which do not exemplify the connection between desire and action. But, though this is the right description of the result, it leaves us in the original difficulty, that, when the result is described in this way, the desire seems to be its logically sufficient condition, given the background conditions (which now do not include the agent's factual belief, because it has been accommodated at another point).

It is evidently no good trying to avoid this difficulty by analysing the desire to shoot the rabbit into its components. For whatever the composition of the desire to shoot the rabbit, it must be strong enough under that description to produce the action under the matching description. A more promising line would be to examine the thesis that it is an analytic statement that, if a person really wants to do a particular thing, he will do it given certain background conditions, in order to see if it is defensible. So far it has been conceded validity without defence.

It could be attacked on the ground that, though we are all familiar with factors which must appear on the list of background conditions – for instance, it must be stipulated that performance be possible, and be believed by the agent to be possible – nobody has yet produced a complete list which yields an acceptable analytic statement. Whatever familiar conditions were known to be fulfilled in a given case, we might still find it conceivable that the person really did want to perform the action, in spite of the fact that he did not perform it, perhaps because there might have been an impediment of a kind with which we are not yet familiar. This suggests that, when we use a closed list of background conditions and get a negative result, we ought to conclude only that it was improbable – perhaps highly improbable – that the agent really did want to perform the action. There may be further factors waiting to be discovered, which would give us a knockdown necessary condition of really wanting to perform an action, if we discovered them and included them in our list. But even if it is theoretically necessary that there should be such further factors, the behavioural criterion which we actually use is not knockdown.

This is a powerful attack on simple versions of logical

behaviourism. It makes a considerable impact on the thesis that, if a person really wants to do a thing, he will do it given certain background conditions. Let us analyse its strategy.

First, it is clear that, if it is successful, it will not get rid of my problem, but will only force me to restate it. For whatever the list of the background conditions in the behavioural criterion, and however relaxed the type of connection between the desire and the behavioural criterion may be – if revisable analyticity is too rigid, it may be criterial contingency – it is difficult to see how we can say that the desire produces the action unless the desire can be given some further description which satisfies the Humean requirement. So I shall treat the list of background conditions as a variable in this discussion, and I shall call the total result – i.e., action given the background conditions – "the behavioural result." Also when I refer to criterial connections I shall leave it an open question whether the statements that report them are analytic (but revisable), or not.

Let me now look at the detailed moves in the attack on the excessively simple version of logical behaviourism. It is suggested that, whatever closed list of background conditions we use, if we get a negative result by the behavioural criterion, we might still find it conceivable that the person had really wanted to perform the action. This is true, and the explanation of it is that we have a second criterion of really wanting to perform an action, the agent's sincere say-so, which is, if anything, a logically sufficient condition of such a desire. We feel the pull of this antecedent criterion in cases in which it conflicts with the behavioural criterion, and we realize that, whatever refinements may be introduced into the behavioural criterion, we might still allow the antecedent criterion to win in cases of conflict.

We might. But would we? This is a hard question to answer. All that is really certain is that it cannot be the case both that the agent's sincere say so is a logically and universally sufficient condition of the desire to perform an action, and that the behavioural result is a logically and universally necessary condition of it. This cannot be the case, whatever list of background conditions is put into the behavioural criterion. But it is less certain what would in fact happen in cases of conflict. There might be refinements of the behavioural criterion, based on new psychological discoveries, which would lead us to allow it to win in all cases of conflict. On the other hand, if we used a very rough behavioural criterion, we might allow the antecedent criterion to win in all cases of conflict. The best behavioural criterion which is available at the moment seems to take us down the middle road between these two extremes, allowing neither criterion to dominate the other completely.

But all this is problematic. What is certain is that, if it is a fact that the agent's sincere say-so is always followed by the behavioural result, it is a contingent fact. More generally, whatever the proportion of cases in which it is followed by the behavioural result, it is a contingent fact that the proportion is what it is. This generalization is important, because it shows that, even if, instead of making the connection between either, or both, the criteria and the desire a universal connection, we made it a high statistical connection, there would still be the contingent possibility of a conflict between the two criteria. For instance, we might realize that, if we treated both criteria as knockdown, the concept of a desire to perform an action would be a hopeless hostage to fortune, and so we might write into each of the two criteria a percentage which was something less than one hundred. If we did this, a radical conflict – i.e., the sort of conflict which might jeopardize the concept – would not be a single case in which a person's sincere say-so was not followed by the behavioural result, but would be a certain proportion of cases in which this happened. But a radical conflict would still be contingently possible.

The antecedent criterion obviously holds out some hope of a solution to my problem. If we did not have it, the question, whether the desire to perform a particular action can be described in a way that satisfies the Humean requirement, could only be given a speculative answer. We could only speculate that it is satisfied, perhaps by some physical description of brain-states which may be discovered one day. But the fact that we have the antecedent criterion offers some hope that it is not ignorance, but lack of ingenuity, which makes it difficult to produce a description of the desire which satisfies the Humean requirement. For it may be that this criterion contains all the material that we need for the task. It may be that, if we analyze it, we shall find a description of the desire under which it is a contingently sufficient condition of the behavioural result. As I pointed out earlier, it is hard to believe that we should need to make a further scientific discovery before we would be in a position to produce such a description of the desire. For the agent's knowledge that he will do a particular thing is often based on his present desire.

Is it possible to extract from the antecedent criterion a description of the desire which satisfies the Humean requirement? Here it must be remembered that what makes this task difficult is not the fact that the description of the desire has to mention its object, but, rather, the fact that it has to specify its strength. The trouble is that, when we apply Hume's razor, and pare away any specification of its strength which has the behavioural result as the criterially necessary condition of its application, there is so little left. Apparently all that is left is the description, "Desire of a strength which justifies the agent's claim that he really wants to perform the action." So let us ask whether this description satisfies the Humean requirement.

It might be argued that it does not satisfy it, because the agent's claim could not be justified unless his desire passed the test of the behavioural criterion (whatever the list of background conditions, and whatever the type of criterial connection may be). But it is possible to answer this argument by using Hume's razor on the concept of justification, and distinguishing between a reasonable, but possibly incorrect claim, and a claim that is both reasonable and correct. If the word "justified" is used in the first way, the desire under the suggested description is a contingently sufficient condition of the behavioural result.

But at this point it might be objected that the description, taken in this way, selects the wrong class of cases. It ought to select cases of really wanting to perform actions, but instead it selects cases which are reasonably believed by the agent to be such cases. This is the wrong class, because it includes cases in which the agent's claim, that he really wants to perform the action, is incorrect, and because it excludes unconscious desires.

I shall not take up the point about unconscious desires, because it is the other charge – that the class includes cases which it ought to exclude – which would be damaging if it were valid. It would be damaging, because I am trying to find a description of the desire to perform a particular action under which it is a contingently sufficient condition of the behavioural result, and a description which includes cases which are not cases of genuine desires to perform actions will not fill the bill. The fact that the description excludes unconscious desires does not matter in this context. If there are two kinds of desires, conscious desires and unconscious desires, each of which is a sufficient condition of the behavioural result, there can be no objection to restricting this inquiry to one of those two sufficient conditions.

It is important to observe that the damaging charge can be generalized. The trouble is not merely that the suggested description includes cases in which the behavioural result does not follow. That would be a fault if it were a criterially necessary condition of genuine desires to perform actions that the behavioural results should always follow. But even if a lower criterial percentage is adopted, the thesis is still vulnerable to a generalized version of the objection, viz., that, whatever behavioural criterion is adopted, if the suggested description includes cases in which the agent's claim, that he really wants to do a particular thing, turns out to be incorrect when it is judged by the behavioural criterion, then it will include cases which are not cases of really wanting to do that thing.

But the objection is invalid both in its original version and in its generalized version. It is easier to see what is wrong with the original version of it. The objector assumes that it is a criterially necessary condition of genuine desires to perform actions that the behavioural results should always follow. He also assumes that, when the agent sincerely claims that he really wants to do a particular thing, that is a criterially and universally sufficient condition of the fact that his desire is of a strength which justifies his claim. But these are, as it were, fair weather assumptions. If the antecedents and behavioural criteria never came into conflict, they would cause no trouble. But the objector is extending the assumptions to cases of conflict, in order to drive a wedge between really wanting to perform an action and having a desire of a strength which justifies the claim to really want to perform it. For the theory which he is attacking equates these two things, and would maintain their identity even in cases of conflict. So the answer to the objection is to refuse to allow this wedge to be driven between them in cases of conflict. All that is necessary is to deny that the behavioural result is a criterially and universally necessary condition of really wanting to perform a particular action, and to maintain that, when the behavioural result does not follow, if this is taken to indicate that the agent did not really want to perform the action, then it also indicates that his desire was not of the strength which would justify his claim that he really did want to perform it.

The answer to the generalized version of the objection follows the same lines. The objector assumes that it is a criterially necessary condition of really wanting to perform an action that the behavioural result should nearly always follow. Then it is equally easy to refuse to allow a wedge to be driven between really wanting to perform an action and having a desire of a strength which justifies the claim to really want to perform it. The only difference is that the background to the refusal is rather more complex on the current supposition. The background is the following: The correlation between the behavioural criterion and genuine desires to perform actions is nearly exceptionless, and the same is true of the antecedent criterion. Since each criterion allows some latitude, there may well be conflicts of a kind which would not jeopardize the concept of really wanting to perform an action (non-radical conflicts). There may also be more frequent conflicts which would jeopardize the concept (radical conflicts). In both kinds of conflict alike we only need to refuse to attach the concept of a desire of a strength which justifies the claim to really want to perform an action any more closely to the antecedent criterion than we would attach the concept of a genuine desire to perform it to the antecedent criterion. For these two concepts are, according to the thesis which is here being defended, identical.

At this point it might be objected that I have not allowed for the general dominance of the behavioural criterion. For I have taken a situation in which the concept of desire to perform a particular action has already been set up in a workable way, and I have argued that in such a situation, when the two criteria conflict radically or non-radically, victory would be conceded sometimes to one and sometimes to the other, and, of course, sometimes the issue would be left undecided. In this way I seem to have reached the conclusion that there is a description of such desires under which they are the contingently sufficient conditions of the behavioural results. But the conflicts envisaged would only be occasional conflicts. If I had examined the effect of a protracted radical conflict between the two criteria, I would have noticed that the behavioural criterion dominates the antecedent criterion in a way which upsets my conclusion. If, for example, tomorrow in this country the proportion of cases in which the behavioural criterion was fulfilled after the antecedent criterion had been fulfilled suddenly dropped almost to zero, and stayed there, the antecedent criterion would simply be denied criterial status. This shows that the behavioural criterion is generally dominant. So when I use the antecedent criterion as the source of a description which satisfies the Humean requirement, I ought not to claim that the concept of desire to perform a particular action is more or less equally balanced between the two criteria. If there were a protracted radical conflict, it would simply detach itself from the antecedent criterion, and in that case there really would be a wedge driven between really wanting to perform a particular action and having a desire which justified the claim that one really wanted to perform it.

One step towards answering this objection would be to draw a further distinction within the concept of a justified claim. A distinction has already been drawn between a reasonable, but possibly incorrect, claim, and a claim which is both reasonable and correct. Now the phrase "reasonable, but possibly incorrect, claim" was intended to allow for possible occasional conflicts between the two criteria. We now need a further distinction which will allow for the onset of a protracted radical conflict between them. We must distinguish between claims which are justified by a desire (but possibly incorrect, because of occasional conflicts), because either they are made before the onset of a protracted radical conflict, or, if they are made after it, the person who makes the claim is not aware of the onset of such a conflict, and claims which would be justified in this way if either of these two conditions were fulfilled, but which are not justified in this way because neither is fulfilled. Let me express this distinction in a simpler way before I apply it. There is a certain strength of desire which, before the onset of a protracted radical conflict, or after it, but before the agent is aware of it, justifies his claim that he really wants to perform the action (though he knows that when such claims are judged by the behavioural criterion they are occasionally rejected): but a claim, which is based on a desire of this strength after a protracted radical conflict has begun, and after he has become aware that it has begun, is no longer justified in this way.

This distinction can be used to show that the objection which is being considered has no force. For the description of the desire under which it is a contingently sufficient condition of the behavioural result is the description "Desire of a strength which justifies the agent's claim that he really wants to perform the action." If we apply the distinction at this point, and stipulate that the desire be of a strength which justifies the agent's claim only if one of the two conditions given above is fulfilled, the objection is answered. It is true that the behavioural criterion is dominant in a general way, and that this puts a limitation on the situations in which the concept of desire to perform a particular action can be set up and continue to work: if there were no antecedent factor which was reasonably well and durably correlated with the behavioural result, we would not have this concept. But that does not upset my conclusion, which relies on a description of the desire which includes the stipulation that either a protracted radical conflict has not yet begun, or, if it has begun, the agent is not yet aware of it.

But there are other possible objections which might be made against my way of extracting from the antecedent criterion a description of desires to perform actions under which they are contingently sufficient conditions of the behavioural results. I shall end this paper by mentioning, and dealing with, three of them.

First, there is a well known difficulty about verifiability. Let us give the name "adequate" to the strength of desire which, provided that one of the two conditions given above is fulfilled, justifies the agent's claim that he really wants to perform the action. Then it may be objected that, if the antecedent and behavioural criteria came into conflict, it would be an unverifiable, and therefore empty, hypothesis, that the actual strength of the person's desire had been adequate, or that it had not been adequate. Suppose, for example, that the conflict happened to you: then you could say either that the strength of your desire had been adequate, or that it had not been adequate and that your memory had tricked you on this point. Now if neither hypothesis is verifiable, both are empty. But according to my account of the relationship between the two criteria, in cases of conflict we would sometimes allow one criterion to win and sometimes the other (and sometimes neither). The short answer to this objection is that knockdown verification is not necessary, and that it is not true that there is no possible evidence that would discriminate between the two hypotheses in a case of conflict. For example, one obviously necessary background condition in the behavioural criterion is psychological possibility, and a group of cases of conflict might be explained by the diagnosis of a new psychological syndrome which made certain actions psychologically impossible. Such a discovery would not actually add a new background condition to the list, but it would add something to the criterion of an already listed background condition. It is true that its effect would not be to establish in a knockdown way that, in the cases examined, the strength of desire had been adequate, but it would make it improbable that the patients were mistaken in thinking it adequate.

However, this kind of example does not really get rid of the objection, because it introduces a change in the behavioural criterion. The real difficulty occurs when both criteria are kept unchanged, because there is no protracted radical conflict, but only occasional conflicts. But even here we may have indications which point to one hypothesis rather than the other. For instance, there might be evidence that the agent was likely to deceive himself and exaggerate the strength of his desire. But a full answer to this objection would require space for a detailed examination of different cases.

Another objection would be that my account implies that the agent uses a criterion when he judges the strength of his desire to perform a particular action, whereas in fact his judgment (if it can be called that) is immediate, and not based on any criterion. But this objection is produced by a misunderstanding. My account of the relationship between the antecedent criterion and the behavioural criterion is far from implying that the agent himself uses a criterion. First, as was pointed out near the beginning of this paper, the agent's say-so is not always based on his present desire. It may be the sole present manifestation of his desire construed as a disposition. But second, even when it is based on his present desire, because he reflects, and asks himself whether he does really want to perform the action, nothing that I have said implies that he uses a criterion in order to arrive at the answer. It is true that, if he says that he does, he will say this because he thinks that his desire is adequate, and, if he thinks that it is adequate, he will think this because it seems to him to be adequate. But these two steps are too short to count as backward steps to criteria. In any case, my account leaves the question, whether these are criteria for the agent or not, open, because, though it says that there is a description of his desire which satisfies the Humean requirement, it does not imply that the agent himself uses this description as a criterion.

A third objection to my way of extracting this description from the antecedent criterion would be that it implies that the agent learned to recognize the adequate strength of a desire by waiting to see if the behavioural result occurred, and that, in the early stages of learning, the various strengths of his desires were problematic data, which he did not quite know how to interpret. But this objection too is based on a misunderstanding. For my account of the two criteria implies nothing about the way in which the concept of desire to perform a particular action is acquired. It only implies that the concept, when we have it, can be taken to pieces in the way that has been outlined.

So my solution to the second problem is that, when desires are taken as sufficient conditions of actions, given the background conditions, the Humean requirement can certainly be satisfied; whereas my solution to the first problem was that, when they are taken as necessary conditions of actions, it may be satisfiable. This does not show that desires are causes of actions. Nor does it show that there is nothing which ought to lead us to treat the connection between desires and actions as a special kind of connection. All that it shows is that the idea that the Humean requirement cannot be satisfied, and that this ought to lead us to treat the connection in a special way, is an illusion.

There is one final point which I would like to make. If the desire to do A has a description under which it is a contingently sufficient condition of the behavioural result, then it is possible that, when someone says that he did A just because he felt like it, this singular statement entails the contingent general statement, that the same behavioural result will follow whenever he feels as much like doing A. It is also possible that, in cases in which he analyses his desire to do A into various component desires, his singular statement entails the contingent general statement, that the same behavioural result will follow whenever he feels those component desires to the same degree. Now in this paper I have used an argument about the agent's foreknowledge of his action which supports the thesis that these contingent general statements really are entailed by the relevant singular statements. But in order to establish the thesis, it would be necessary to examine in detail the ways in which such singular statements are falsified, and I have not attempted to carry out that task in this paper.

F

Comments

BY IRVING THALBERG

I INTERPRETING PEARS'S QUESTIONS

When we investigate human behaviour, we commonly ask both what a person is doing and why. Men's deeds and their grounds for acting appear to be distinct phenomena. They must be, if one's attitudes and thoughts ever cause one to act. Yet, as Professor Pears reminds us, we often specify what a man is doing in terms that seem to entail that he had some particular reason for doing it; and conversely, if we limit ourselves to reporting someone's conative attitudes, we nevertheless seem to be providing information about how he will act in favourable circumstances. The descriptions by which we identify a man's action and its psychological antecedents seem to create logical ties between them. Pears illustrates this predicament by supposing that we correctly describe someone as shooting a rabbit. If we assume that his performance was in some sense "intentional," doesn't it follow logically that he had some kind of desire to shoot the rabbit? Surely he wanted to, craved to, or just felt he would like to shoot it? And from the converse side, Pears remarks that "it may be hard to see how his desire, described in this way, given certain background conditions, one of which will be his factual beliefs, could possibly have failed to produce his action, as originally described" (p. 129).

This is the ground-floor level of Pears's two problems. I take him to be asking: (a) Is it a *logically necessary* condition of someone's doing X that he desires to do X? In other words, does the action statement, "N does X," entail "N desires to do X"? (b) Is it a *logically sufficient* condition of someone's doing X that, in favorable circumstances, he desires to do X? That is, will "N desires to do X," together with suitable background assumptions regarding N's other desires, his abilities, opportunities, means, rights, and information, entail "*N* does *X*"?

On this level, Pears's goals are to establish: (α) that desires are not logically necessary conditions of actions, (β) that desires are not logically sufficient conditions of actions. Incidentally, his theses (α) and (β) are entirely compatible with all of the following widely held theses about the logical ties between desire and action:

Tγ "*N* does *X* intentionally" entails that there is some true description of *X* such that, under that description, *N* desires to do *X*.[1]

Tδ "*N* does *X*" and "*N* tells us that he is doing *X* intentionally" entail "*N* desires to do *X*."

Tϵ We never know for certain that a descriptive statement of the form, "*N* does *X* intentionally," is true, until we know (from *N*'s avowal, for instance) that *N* wants to do *X*.

T$\varkappa$ We never know for certain what a person's desires are until we have evidence regarding his overt behaviour.

Tλ The concept of desire for an end is embedded in our concept of intentional or purposive behaviour.

Tμ We have the concept of desiring only because we know what actions count as evidence, or natural expressions of various kinds of desire.[2]

I will deal with Pears's two problems only on this ground-floor level. Most of his argument, however, proceeds on a higher level. For he immediately begins asking: (a′) Is it a *contingently necessary* condition of someone's doing *X* that

---

1 I adopt this formulation from Donald Davidson's paper, "Agency." My general approach to the problem of describing actions is greatly influenced by Davidson. However, he may not agree with the conclusions I reach here.

2 Theses Tλ and Tμ are prominent, and persuasively argued, in A. I. Melden's *Free Action* (London: Routledge & Kegan Paul, 1961); unfortunately Melden seems at times to confuse them with the contentions at issue here, namely that instances of desire and instances of action are logically connected (see pp. 16, 17, 46, 53, 76, 77, 88–90, 110–136, 152, 158, 170, 196, 200, 203).

F*

he desires to do *X*? (b') Is it a *contingently sufficient* condition of someone's doing *X* in favourable circumstances that he
desires to do *X*? On this higher level, which is really the
locus of his interest, Pears endeavours to meet what he calls a
general "Humean requirement" for saying that one event is
a contingently necessary or sufficient condition of another.
Pears' Humean demand is rigorous: we must furnish
identifying descriptions of each particular action and the
agent's desire "under which they are universally and contingently connected" (p. 130). His higher-level goals are thus
to prove that desires are (α') contingently necessary and (β')
contingently sufficient for the deeds they accompany.

The difference between questions (a) and (b) and Pears's
higher-level questions is obvious. But one could easily
confuse the ground-floor tasks (α) and (β) with Pears's main
goals (α') and (β'). The corresponding predicates,

   "… are not logically necessary (or sufficient) conditions of ---,"
   "… are contingently necessary (or sufficient) conditions of ---,"

sound nearly synonymous. But the former actually means:

   "It is not the case that … are logically necessary (or sufficient)
   conditions of ---."

So understood, the corresponding phrases in (α) and (α') and
in (β) and (β'), are not even extensionally equivalent. For instance, when John smokes and paces, his pacing is not a
logically necessary or logically sufficient condition of his
smoking. It is not inconsistent to suppose that he does one
and not the other. But from this it hardly follows that John's
pacing is a contingently necessary or sufficient condition of
his smoking!

Why bother distinguishing these two levels of Pears's
problems, and why concentrate on their ground-floor aspects,
if his concern is with the higher-level aspects of his problems?
One reason is that, in the course of Pears's dialectical reply to
his higher-level questions, he often reaches a negative con-

clusion, namely that a certain desire is not a contingently necessary or sufficient condition of a particular action, *because* the desire appears to be a logically necessary or sufficient condition of the deed (pp. 133, 138, 142). Therefore, although Pears himself thinks the ground-floor questions (a) and (b) are easy to dispose of, they give him trouble when he deals with his higher-level questions (a') and (b').

Another reason why I strain to keep the levels of his inquiry straight is that I want to confine Pears's "Humean requirement" to the upper-level inquiry. For suppose we wish to demonstrate that the particular longing you had this afternoon, when you ordered a chocolate eclair for tea, is (α) neither a logically necessary, (β) nor a logically sufficient, condition of your behaviour. Then all we have to do is contrive logically independent identifying descriptions of those two historical occurrences. We certainly do not have to meet Pears's Humean demand that we describe those episodes in such a way that, every time *another* desire occurs which meets our desire-description, it will also accompany *another* deed which fulfills our original action-description, and conversely. From the fact that the two episodes were not logically connected, we cannot infer that similar episodes will always be found together.

Finally, I concentrate on Pears's ground-floor questions (a) and (b) because I think they should have given him much less trouble. So, instead of evaluating Pears's ingenious and thorough answers to his higher-level questions (a') and (b'), I will devote the rest of this paper to criticizing a few assumptions he makes which give us the mistaken impression that his ground-floor questions are pretty tough. In particular, these assumptions seem to lead him to neglect quite simple proofs that individual actions and desires are not logically connected. What is more, these misconceptions I find in Pears's discussion are interesting and tempting, and they pervade many other top-flight philosophical works on action. These misconceptions have to do with three overlapping topics: what sorts of occurrences qualify as actions, generally speaking; what it is for an event to be an intentional action; and what it is to give identifying descriptions of events that happen to be instances of a person desiring something or doing something.

II ACTIONS WITHOUT DESIRE

Pears's first mistake, with regard to question (a), is that he neglects actions we perform without wanting or intending to in any way. Examples would be: spontaneous and unreflective actions like cavorting in the ocean; habitual and routine tasks; automatic gestures like shaking hands; many of the facial expressions we assume; various compulsive movements we execute, usually unawares. I won't even mention actions that in one respect we want to perform, but in another respect do not want to perform: for instance when we act under compulsion or duress; when we are hypnotized; or when by error or accident we bring about an unwanted result. If we broaden our concept of action to encompass the other cases, then we have an obvious group of actions which are never characterized by reference to the agent's desires or purposes. For instance: when a factory worker is busy at the assembly line, it is incorrect to infer that he wants or intends to be executing each of the rote actions we observe. And it will not do to say that all we see are bodily movements or processes. There is a world of difference between his digesting his lunch, which is a mere bodily process, and his activity on the assembly line.[3]

Another range of cases where we identify events as actions of a given type, but need not suppose that the agent desired in

3 Here is one of several differences I spell out in "Verbs, Deeds, and What Happens to Us," *Theoria*, 33, no. 3 (1966), 264–268. As things stand, it makes no sense to report that someone digested his lunch on purpose, by accident, deliberately, unintentionally, and so on; by contrast, it is always intelligible to say these things about the worker's rote gestures. In Pears's terminology, a rote action could have, but a bodily process could not have, issued from the agent's desire.

any way to perform them, is created by some social conventions. Here's a far-fetched illustration. I am touring an exotic country. I get lost, and, having no idea where I am going, I blunder unwittingly into a cemetery. I have desecrated the place, and, as I flee, the natives have to purify it. I have desecrated the cemetery although I had no desire even to enter it, and no inkling of what the natives count as profaning a sacred locality.

Now we should look at Pears's homelier example of someone shooting a rabbit. Will our identifying description of the incident always imply that the rabbit-shooter has a desire? Not at all. Here's a neutral account of the episode. You observe a waking man with full control of his limbs. He has a rifle in his hands. His index finger closes on the trigger. A rabbit is hit. He shot the rabbit. Did he desire or intend this? To begin with, it is possible that he had no relevant desire or intention. Perhaps he has a nervous habit of clenching and unclenching his fists, and he unwittingly did so while holding the rifle. This tripped the firing mechanism, and the rabbit was struck. In other words, possibly his action falls into the category of frowns, tics, routine and compulsive gestures which I said Pears overlooked.

Alternatively, the marksman had a desire, but not the desire to shoot this rabbit. Here are some possibilities: he wanted to test the rifle, and did not see that there was a rabbit in his line of fire; he saw the rabbit, but mistook it for a bothersome gopher; he recognized the rabbit, but only wanted to scare it away; he was aiming at a target, and believed the rabbit was safely out of range; he was trying to get another rabbit, and winged this one by mistake. In all these situations, it is true to report that our protagonist shot the rabbit. The shooting is also now an intentional act. In Davidson's terms, there is a true description of the shooting under which the agent intended to be acting.[4] Yet it is not true, and hence not a logical consequence of our statements

4 See footnote 1 above.

describing the action, that the fellow desired or intended to shoot that rabbit as he did.[5]

My criticism may sound unfair to Pears's illustration. For he imagines that the nimrod has supplied us with matching descriptions of his act and his desire. But why must we prefer the agent's description of his behaviour to the neutral ones I started with? First of all, his report might be erroneous. Perhaps he cannot honestly misdescribe his desire; however, with regard to his actual performance, his description can be deficient in many ways. It may be inaccurate or mistaken, or both, for him to assert that he has succeeded in *doing* what he wanted to do. For all he knows, his bullet might have blown his prey to bits, and it might have struck more than one rabbit. It might have missed altogether; possibly the rabbit is just playing dead. So we are in as good a position as the agent to describe what he has accomplished. Furthermore, even if his account is impeccable, we are still entitled to describe his action in the neutral terms I used, which do not imply that he intended or wanted to shoot the rabbit.

III THE CONTINGENCY OF INTENTIONS

Why does Pears think that once the agent has informed us of his desire or intention in acting, we must stick to that characterization of what he did? My hypothesis is that, despite the scruples he expresses at several junctures (pp. 130, 133, 134), Pears believes that, if it is true to describe an action as done with some intention, then it is necessarily true, no matter how you describe the incident, that the agent had that intention when he acted as he did. Pears argues:

Whatever the composition of his desire to shoot it, if he shot it

---

5 Pears considers this line of argument on pp. 130–134; but he restricts himself to alternative desires, such as the desire to eat the rabbit, which happen to be logically bound up with shooting it in the circumstances.

intentionally, his shooting it must have issued from that desire ... [T]he statement that his desire to shoot it, whatever its composition, was a necessary condition of his shooting it ... is not contingent as it stands, and it is difficult to see what alternative description of the action would turn it into a contingent statement (p. 133).

My objection is that it is a contingent fact about the agent that he had the particular intention of shooting that rabbit. As I illustrated in the previous section, it could still be true to describe him as shooting the rabbit, even if he had no intention or had the other intentions I listed. The only necessity here comes from our description of the action as an intentional shooting; this description, and not the occurrence of the act, entails that the agent intended to shoot the rabbit. But it is not necessary that we identify the action by that description. In the next section I will examine the assumptions which seem to lead Pears, and many other leading writers on action, to think that we must identify the action by the description under which it was intentional for the agent.

At this stage I want to see how things stand with Pears's ground-level questions (a) and (b). My three groups of elementary counter-examples take care of (a) by showing that action-statements do not entail desire-statements. How do they affect (b)? For the sake of argument, assume that the only way we characterize desire is as "that which is accompanied by action in favourable circumstances, and is avowed by the agent to be his desire."[6] Remaining with Pears's example, the hunter's desire to shoot a particular rabbit would be whatever is accompanied by his attempting to shoot it, and

---

6 The situation would be partly analogous to the following imaginary predicament. Suppose that the only way we can describe fuel is as "that which makes engines run, heats things, and so on"; disinfectant is known only as "that which kills germs"; solvents are "what causes solid objects to dissolve"; soporifics are "what produce sleep." In the case of desire, our predicament would be that we can only identify it by reference to its effects and the avowals which are taken as evidence of desire.

whatever he is avowing. This description of his attitude does not entail that he succeeds in shooting it, for he might miss or hit another rabbit; nor does it entail any of the more specific statements which I used to describe his performance in the preceding section. Therefore the rabbit-shooter's desire is not a logically sufficient condition of his actual detailed performance.[7]

Does my line of reply to Pears's ground-floor questions (a) and (b) demonstrate that desires and actions are distinct or separate events? It shows that when both occur, they are separable, and it shows that actions occur without desires. I have not proven, and I do not think Pears has either, that desires may occur on their own. They could be supervenient occurrences. It is compatible with everything I have asserted so far, to maintain that when we report a person's desire, we are reporting his manner of acting, especially his manner during preparatory behaviour. To say that a man has a desire would be to say that he does something; for example, he engages in various forms of preference behaviour, or he gets ready to play golf, to visit friends, to seduce a blonde, in a desiring manner – avidly, enthusiastically, determinedly, eagerly, lustfully, or whatnot.

Rather than develop these speculative answers to Pears's sufficient-condition question (b), I want to close by examining another line of argument, directed to (a) and (a′), which Pears finds inadequate. His reasoning brings out very clearly some important and tempting misconceptions of what it is to describe actions and desires.

IV IDENTIFYING AND IDENTIFYING AS

The line of reasoning considered by Pears is more radical than the methods for identifying actions that I propounded in Section II above. Still the same goal is attained, of identifying

7 Pears notices but rejects this line of reply to (b), pp. 140–142.

what an agent did through a description that implies nothing about the agent's desires or intentions. We simply record his bodily movements while he acted. I am sure Pears would allow us to construe "bodily movement" broadly, so that even when the agent's limbs are motionless, and his posture and position do not alter, it would nevertheless be true to say that his body moved. For he might be acting at the time: hiding, waiting, or relaxing. Hence the proposal is: we report a particular deed by specifying enough of the agent's bodily movements, together with their spatio-temporal features, to enable a listener to single out the action to which they belong from other events in the neighbourhood.

What's wrong with this method? One objection Pears notices is that "a physical description of [the action] A would be a description of A as a bodily movement and not ... as the action of A" (p. 135). Pears qualifies and strengthens this objection by asserting:

> A description of A by its physical characteristics might apply only if it were A [only if every event with those characteristics would be the same type of action as A?]. Such a description would be a description of it as the action A, in the relevant sense of the phrase ... Perhaps we ought to stipulate that the description must be a description of A by its intrinsic physical characteristics, in order to exclude descriptions which bring in antecedent brain states, because descriptions which did that might be thought to bring in desires (p. 135).

Thus if Pears's "physical" description of A "as the action A" is to identify A through the agent's bodily movements, it must record the physical features which every action of the same kind shares with A. This is the most plausible interpretation of the above reasoning. It also accords with the next explicit step in Pears's reply. Pears goes on to stiffen his requirement for a physical description of the action A "as the action A": it must include a general "description of those bodily movements which are actions" (p. 135). Given these demands, it is hardly surprising when Pears turns down the proposal to identify actions through the bodily movements they comprise. He argues:

> We [lack] ... the general ability to distinguish between those bodily movements which are actions and those which are mere bodily movements, without using as a criterion the presence or absence of the relevant desire ... If we had the general ability ... , it could be argued that ... [we have] the material out of which we could construct a description which would satisfy the Humean requirement. But we do not have this general ability (p. 136).

Evidently Pears shifts from the question (a), whether desire is a logically necessary condition of action, to (a'), whether desire is a contingently necessary condition.[8] Quite apart from this minor confusion, he assimilates the easy job of identifying a particular action of kind K, to the nearly hopeless job of identifying all actions that belong to type K; then he adds the impossible task of specifying bodily movements that actions of type K and every other type have in common.

I think Pears's demands are illegitimate. We can identify an occurrence which is an action through any description, physiological or otherwise, that singles it out. We don't have to list those characteristics, if any, which identify that particular event as an instance of K-type action. Why should there even be any? A type of action, like shooting or swimming, may be performed in various fashions. People swim by doing the dog-paddle, the crawl; they stay on the surface or go underwater; and so forth. If we can use all these quite different action-terms to characterize instances of an action like swimming, why assume that the same bodily-movement terms will fit each instance of swimming? And especially why assume that not only every instance of swimming, but every

---

8 He also seems to shift his attention from the doctrine that desires are logically necessary conditions of actions, to the epistemological thesis (τε) which I formulated on p. 155.

occurrence that ranks as an action of any type, will exhibit the same physiological features? I conclude that Pears's argument against neurophysiological identifying descriptions of actions is unsound, because he mistakenly sets too high a standard for a description of an action.

That is all I have to say regarding Pears's assumptions which make his ground-level questions (a) and (b) sound much tougher than they are. I have not attacked his reasoning about the higher-level questions (a') and (b') that mainly concern him. As I said to begin with, I like his treatment of those issues. Still my criticism throughout this paper of Pears's notions of describing might raise some doubts regarding his method of answering (a') and (b'). In particular, Pears's Humean requirement for affirmative answers to (a') and (b') now seems unnecessarily stiff. Let me explain why, by reference to my objections against Pears's view of what it is to give logically independent descriptions of someone's deed and the desire on which he acted.

Pears was wrong to demand that logically independent descriptions be such that, every time a desire occurs which fits our desire-description, an action must occur which meets our action-description, and conversely, whether or not the action is described in neurophysiological jargon. This demand was illegitimate because there is no reason to assume, *a priori*, that logically distinct kinds of events will always be found together. The moral for Pears's upper-level problems is straightforward. Just because a desire of type W was a contingently necessary or sufficient condition, in favourable circumstances, for an action of type K, does it follow that desires and actions of these kinds will always consort with each other? My hankering for exercise might be a contingently necessary or sufficient condition of extremely varied behaviour while I am favourably located at the gymnasium. My desire is a contingently necessary or sufficient condition of my lifting barbells for a few minutes, then of my running, and finally of my tumbling. And of course we can describe these actions in neutral or in neurophysiological terms, which do not entail that I wanted to exercise. Anyway, if it does not sound self-contradictory to say that my desire is a contingently necessary or sufficient condition, in continuously favourable circumstances, of these quite dissimilar actions, then we have no reason to insist upon Pears's Humean requirement. For it would prohibit us from saying that my desire is a contingently necessary or sufficient condition of my indescribably varied activity. Pears's Humean requirement is not out of place, as it was when we were trying to establish the logical independence of desire and action. It is appropriate now to ask whether the requirement is met. But I am suggesting that, even when the Humean requirement is unsatisfied, a desire might still be a contingently necessary or sufficient condition of what someone does.[9]

9 I benefited from discussing Pears's essay with Pears himself, and with my colleagues Fred Feldman and David Blumenfeld.

5 / A Bibliography of the Philosophy of Action

Robert McGowan and
Myron Gochnauer

This is intended to be a substantial, though not an exhaustive, bibliography of recent work in the philosophy of action. Completeness is impossible, if for no other reason, because the boundaries of the subject are impossible to draw firmly. The strategy here has been to concentrate on work published since the Second World War, and to avoid following the subject too deeply into ethics, philosophy of mind, and other neighbouring branches of philosophy.

The abbreviations of journal titles are, where possible, those of *Philosopher's Index*, and should be obvious without a key. The bibliography is so arranged that each item is uniquely designated by author, date, and, occasionally, alphabetical subscript, as Brown 1963a and Brown 1963b.

ABELSON, RAZIEL. "Taylor's Fatal Fallacy," *Phil. Rev.*, 72 (1963), 93–96
–" 'Because I Want To,' " *Mind*, 74 (1965), 540–553
ACWORTH, RICHARD. "Smart on Free-Will," *Mind*, 72 (1963), 271–272
ADAMS, E. M. "Mr. Hare on the Role of Principles in Deciding," *Mind*, 65 (1956), 78–80
–"Mental Causality," *Mind*, 75 (1966), 552–563
AIKEN, H. D. "Moral Reasoning," *Ethics*, 64 (1953–54), 24–37
– *Reason and Conduct*. New York: Knopf, 1962
ALDRICH, VIRGIL C. "Behavior, Simulating and Nonsimulating," *J. Phil.*, 63 (1966), 453–457

–"On Seeing Bodily Movements as Actions," *Amer. Phil. Quart.*, 4 (1967), 222–230

ALEXANDER, PETER. "Rational Behavior and Psychoanalytic Explanation," *Mind*, 71 (1962), 326–341

ALEXANDER, PETER and ALISDAIR MACINTYRE. "Symposium: Cause and Cure in Psychotherapy," *Proc. Arist. Soc. Supp.*, 29 (1955), 25–28

ALKER, HENRY. "Will Power," *Analysis*, 21 (1960–61), 78–81

ALLAN, D. J. "Causality, Ancient and Modern," *Proc. Arist. Soc. Supp.*, 39 (1965), 1–18

ALLEN, HAROLD J. "A Logical Condition for the Redescription of Actions in Terms of Their Consequences," *J. Value Inq.*, I (1967), 132–134

ALSTON, WILLIAM. "Wants, Actions, and Causal Explanation" [with comments by Keith Lehrer and rejoinder], in Castañeda, 1967, pp. 301–356

AMBROSE, ALICE. "Austin's 'Philosophical Papers,' " *Philosophy*, 38 (1963), 201–216

ANDO, TAKATURA. *Aristotle's Theory of Practical Cognition*, 2nd ed. The Hague: Martinus Nijhoff, 1965

ANSCOMBE, G. E. M. "Intention," *Proc. Arist. Soc.*, 57 (1956–57), 321–332

– *Intention*. Oxford: Blackwell, 1957

–"The Two Kinds of Error in Action," *J. Phil.*, 60 (1963), 393–401

ANSCOMBE, G. E. M. and J. L. AUSTIN. "Symposium: Pretending," *Proc. Arist. Soc. Supp.*, 32 (1958), 261–294

ARDAL, P. S. "Motives, Intentions and Responsibility," *Phil. Quart.*, 15 (1965), 146–154

ASCHENBRENNER, KARL. "The Roots of Conflict and Action," *Inquiry*, 7 (1964), 245–267

AUNE, BRUCE. "Fatalism and Professor Taylor," *Phil. Rev.*, 71 (1962), 512–519

–"Abilities, Modalities and Free Will," *Phil. Phenomenol. Res.*, 23 (1962–63), 397–413

–"Hypotheticals and Can, Another Look," *Analysis*, 27 (1967), 191–195

AUSTIN, J. L., ed. "What Sort of 'If' Is the 'If' in 'I Can *if* I

Choose?' " [*Analysis* Problem No. 1.], *Analysis*, 12 (1951–52), 125–132 [contributions by "Cuckoo," Brian Ellis, Douglas Gaskings, G. M. Matthews]
- *Ifs and Cans*. London: Oxford University Press, 1956. Reprinted in Austin, 1961, pp. 153–180
-"A Plea for Excuses," *Proc. Arist. Soc.*, 57 (1956–57), 1–30
- See Anscombe and Austin, 1958
- *Philosophical Papers*. Oxford: Oxford University Press, 1961
-"Three Ways of Spilling Ink," *Phil. Rev.*, 75 (1966), 427–440
AYERS, M. R. "Austin on 'Could' and 'Could Have,' " *Phil. Quart.*, 16 (1966), 113–120
- *The Refutation of Determinism*. London: Methuen, 1968

BAIER, KURT. "Good Reasons," *Philosophical Studies*, 4 (1953), 1–15
- *The Moral Point of View*. Ithaca, NY: Cornell University Press, 1958
-"Could and Would," *Analysis Supplement*, 23 (1962–63), 20–36
-"Action and Agent," *Monist*, 49 (1965), 183–195
BALMUTH, J. "Psychoanalytic Explanation," *Mind*, 74 (1965), 229–235
BARNES, W. H. F., W. D. FALK, and A. E. DUNCAN-JONES. "Symposium: Intention, Motive and Responsibility," *Proc. Arist. Soc. Supp.*, 19 (1945), 230–288
BAYLIS, C. A. "Rational Preference, Determinism and Moral Obligation," *J. Phil.*, 47 (1950), 57–63
BECK, L. W. "Agent, Actor, Spectator, and Critic," *Monist*, 49 (1965), 167–182
-"Conscious and Unconscious Motives," *Mind*, 75 (1966), 155–179
BEDFORD, ERROL. "Emotions," *Proc. Arist. Soc.*, 57 (1956–57), 281–304
BELL, D. R. "Imperatives and the Will," *Proc. Arist. Soc.*, 66 (1965–66), 129–148
BELNAP, NUEL. See Simon, 1967
BENNETT, DANIEL. "Action, Reason and Purpose," *J. Phil.*, 62 (1965), 85–96
BENNETT, JONATHAN. "Acting and Refraining," *Analysis*, 28 (1967), 30–31

BENSON, JOHN. "The Characterization of Actions and the Virtuous Agent," *Proc. Arist. Soc.*, 63 (1962–63), 251–266

BERGSTRÖM, LARS. *The Alternatives and Consequences of Actions.* Stockholm: Almqvist & Wiksell, 1966

BEROFSKY, BERNARD. "Determinism and the Concept of a Person," *J. Phil.*, 61 (1964), 461–475

–, ed. *Free Will and Determinism.* New York: Harper and Row, 1966

BINKLEY, ROBERT W. "A Theory of Practical Reason," *Phil. Rev.*, 74 (1965), 423–448

– See Simon, 1967

–"The Surprise Examination in Modal Logic," *J. Phil.*, 65 (1968), 127–136

–"Intentionality, Minds and Behaviour," *Noûs*, 3 (1969), 49–60

BLACK, MAX. "The Gap between 'Is' and 'Should,' " *Phil. Rev.*, 73 (1964)

–"Making Something Happen," in Hook, 1958, pp. 31–45

BLOCK, IRVING. "Necessary and Sufficient Condition and Taylor's Argument for Fatalism," *Proc. Inter-American Cong. in Phil.*, 2 (1968), 2–10

BODEN, MARGARET A. "In Reply to Hart and Hampshire," *Mind*, 68 (1959), 256–260

BOGEN, JAMES. "Physical Determinism," in Care and Landesman, 1968, pp. 127–156

BRADLEY, M. C. "A Note on Mr. MacIntyre's *Determinism*," *Mind*, 68 (1959), 521–526

BRADLEY, R. D. "Free Will: Problem or Pseudo-Problem?" *Austl. J. Phil.*, 36 (1958)

–"Must the Future Be What It Is Going to Be?" *Mind*, 68 (1959), 193–208

–"Causality, Fatalism, and Morality," *Mind*, 72 (1963), 191–194

BRAITHWAITE, MARGARET MASTERMAN. See Masterman, Margaret

BRAITHWAITE, R. B. "Common Action towards Different Moral Ends," *Proc. Arist. Soc.*, 53 (1952–53), 29–46

–, ed. "Can I Decide to Do Something Immediately without Trying to Do It Immediately?" [*Analysis* Problem No. 7.], *Analysis*, 16 (1955–56), 1–5 [contributions by "Candidus," Brian Ellis, and Nicholas Rescher]

BRAND, MYLES. "Danto on Basic Actions," *Noûs*, 2 (1968), 187–190

BRANDT, RICHARD and JAEGWON KIM. "Wants as Explanations of Actions," *J. Phil.*, 60 (1963), 425–435

BRAYBROOKE, DAVID, *et al.* "Some Questions for Miss Anscombe about Intention," *Analysis*, 22 (1961–62), 49–54

BROADIE, FREDERICK. "Trying and Doing," *Proc. Arist. Soc.*, 66 (1965–66), 27–40

–"Knowing that I Am Doing," *Phil. Quart.*, 17 (1967), 137–149

BRODBECK, MAY. "Explanation, Prediction, and 'Imperfect' Knowledge," in *Minnesota Studies in the Philosophy of Science*, III, edited by Herbert Feigl and Grover Maxwell. Minneapolis: University of Minnesota Press, 1962. Pp. 231–272

BRONAUGH, RICHARD N. (a) "Freedom as the Absence of an Excuse," *Ethics*, 74 (1963–64), 161–173

– (b) "Uncertainty and Free Choice," *Dialogue*, 2 (1963–64), 446–451

–"The Logic of Ability Judgments," *Phil. Quart.*, 18 (1968), 122–130

BROWN, ROBERT. (a) *Explanation in Social Science*. London: Routledge & Kegan Paul, 1963

– (b) "On Having One's Reasons," *Philosophy*, 38 (1963), 264–271

–"Moods and Motives," *Austl. J. Phil.*, 43 (1965), 277–294

BROWNING, DOUGLAS. "Acts," *Rev. Metaph.*, 14 (1960–61), 3–17

–"The Moral Act," *Phil. Quart.*, 12 (1962), 97–108

– *Act and Agent: An Essay in Philosophical Anthropology.* Coral Gables, Fla: University of Miami Press, 1964

–"The Feeling of Freedom," *Rev. Metaph.*, 18 (1964–65), 123–146

CAHN, STEPHEN. "Fatalistic Arguments," *J. Phil.*, 61 (1964), 295–305

CAMPBELL, C. A. "Is 'Freewill' a Pseudo-Problem?" *Mind*, 60 (1951), 441–465

–"Self-Activity and Its Modes," in H. D. Lewis, ed., *Contemporary British Philosophy, Third Series*. London: George Allen & Unwin, 1956. Pp. 83–115

-"Free Will: A Reply to Mr. Bradley," *Austl. J. Phil.*, 36 (1958), 46–56

-"Moral Libertarianism: A Reply to Mr. Franklin," *Phil. Quart.*, 12 (1962), 337–347

-"Professor Smart on Free Will, Praise and Blame: A Reply," *Mind*, 72 (1963), 400–405

CANFIELD, JOHN. "Determinism, Free Will and the Ace Predicator," *Mind*, 70 (1961), 412–416

-"Knowing about Future Decisions," *Analysis*, 22 (1961–62), 127–129

-"The Compatibility of Free Will and Determinism," *Phil. Rev.*, 71 (1962), 352–368

-"Free Will and Determinism: A Reply," *Phil. Rev.*, 72 (1963), 502–504

CARE, NORMAN S. "On Avowing Reasons," *Mind*, 76 (1967), 208–216

CARE, NORMAN S. and CHARLES LANDESMAN, eds. *Readings in the Theory of Action*. Bloomington: University of Indiana Press, 1968

CARGILE, JAMES. "On Having Reasons," *Analysis*, 26 (1965–66), 189–192

CASTAÑEDA, H.-N. "Outline of a Theory on the General Logical Structure of the Language of Action," *Theoria*, 26 (1960), 151–182

-"The Logic of Change, Action, and Norms," *J. Phil.*, 62 (1965), 333–344

-, ed. (a) *Intentionality, Minds and Perception*. Detroit: Wayne State University Press, 1967

- (b) See Davidson, 1967

CASTAÑEDA, H.-N. and GEORGE NAKHNIKIAN, eds. *Morality and the Language of Conduct*. Detroit: Wayne State University Press, 1965

CASTELL, ALBUREY. *The Self in Philosophy*. New York: Macmillan, 1965

CHAPPELL, V. C. "Causation and the Identification of Action," *J. Phil.*, 60 (1963), 700–701

CHILD, ARTHUR. "Doing and Knowing," *Rev. Metaph.*, 9 (1955–56), 377–390

CHISHOLM, R. M. "What Is It to Act upon a Proposition?" *Analysis*, 22 (1961–62), 1–6

–"The Descriptive Element in the Concept of Action," *J. Phil.*, 61 (1964), 613–625

–"Freedom and Action," in Lehrer, 1966, pp. 11–44

– (a) "He Could Have Done Otherwise," *J. Phil.*, 64 (1967), 409–417. Also in *Philosophy Today No. 1*, edited by Jerry H. Gill. New York: Macmillan, 1968. Pp. 236–249

– (b) See Davidson, 1967b

– (c) See von Wright, 1967

CHOPRA, Y. N. "The Consequences of Human Action," *Proc. Arist. Soc.*, 65 (1964–65), 147–166

CODY, ARTHUR B. (a) "Can A Single Action Have Many Different Descriptions?" *Inquiry*, 10 (1967), 164–180

– (b) "Reply to Mr. Dowling," *Inquiry*, 10 (1967), 449–452

COHEN, MENDEL F. "Motives, Causal Necessity and Moral Accountability," *Austl. J. Phil.*, 42 (1964), 322–334

COHEN, S. MARC. See Matthews, Gareth, and Cohen, 1967

COLEMAN, DON. "Cognition and the Will," *J. Phil.*, 61 (1964), 155–158

COOPER, NEIL. "Some Presuppositions of Moral Judgments," *Mind*, 75 (1966), 45–57

DANTO, ARTHUR. "What We Can Do," *J. Phil.*, 60 (1963), 435–445

– (a) *Analytical Philosophy of History*. Cambridge, Cambridge University Press, 1965

– (b) "Basic Actions," *Amer. Phil. Quart.*, 2 (1965), 141–148

–"Freedom and Forbearance," in Lehrer, 1966, pp. 45–63

DANTO, ARTHUR and S. MORGENBESSER. "Character and Free Will," *J. Phil.*, 54 (1957), 493–505

D'ARCY, ERIC. *Human Acts; An Essay in their Moral Evaluation.* Oxford: Clarendon Press, 1963

DAVENEY, T. F. "Wanting," *Phil. Quart.*, 11 (1961), 135–144

–"Choosing," *Mind*, 73 (1964), 515–526

–"Intentions and Causes," *Analysis*, 27 (1966), 23–28

–"Feelings, Causes and Mr. Myers," *Mind*, 76 (1967), 592–594

DAVIDSON, DONALD. "Actions, Reasons and Causes," *J. Phil.*, 60 (1963), 685–700

G

– (a) "Causal Relations," *J. Phil.*, 64 (1967), 691–703
– (b) "The Logical Form of Action Sentences" [with comments by E. J. Lemmon, H.-N. Castañeda, and R. M. Chisholm, and rejoinder], in Rescher, 1967, pp. 81–120
DAVIDSON, DONALD, PATRICK SUPPES, and SIDNEY SIEGEL. *Decision Making: An Experimental Approach.* Stanford: Stanford University Press, 1957
DAVIS, PHILIP E. " 'Action' and 'Cause of Action,' " *Mind*, 71 (1962), 93–95
DIGGS, B. J. "Technical Ought," *Mind*, 69 (1960), 301–317
–"Rules and Utilitarianism," *Amer. Phil. Quart.*, 1 (1964), 32–44
DODWELL, P. C. "Causes of Behaviour and Explanation in Psychology," *Mind*, 69 (1960), 1–13
DONAGAN, ALAN. "Explanation in History," *Mind*, 66 (1957), 145–164
DONNELLAN, K. S. "Knowing What I Am Doing," *J. Phil.*, 60 (1963), 401–409
– See Feinberg, 1964
DORE, CLEMENT. "On the Meaning of 'Could Have,' " *Analysis*, 23 (1962–63), 41–43
–"Is Free Will Compatible with Determinism?" *Phil. Rev.*, 72 (1963), 500–501
–"More On the Meaning of 'Could Have,' " *Analysis*, 24 (1963–64), 41–43
–"On Being Able to Do Otherwise," *Phil. Quart.*, 16 (1966), 137–145
DOWLING, R. E. "Can an Action Have Many Descriptions?" *Inquiry*, 10 (1967), 447–448
DRAY, WILLIAM. *Laws and Explanation in History.* London: Oxford University Press, 1957
–"Choosing and Doing," *Dialogue*, 1 (1962–63), 129–152
–, ed. *Philosophical Analysis and History.* New York: Harper and Row, 1966
DUGGAN, TIMOTHY and BERNARD GERT. "Voluntary Abilities," *Amer. Phil. Quart.*, 4 (1967), 127–135
DUMMETT, MICHAEL. "Bringing about the Past," *Phil. Rev.*, 73 (1964), 338–359
DUNCAN-JONES, A. E. See Barnes, Falk, and Duncan-Jones, 1945

EARLE, W. See Stallknecht, Wade, and Earle, 1955–56

EBERSOLE, FRANK B. "Free-Choice and the Demands of Morals," *Mind*, 61 (1952), 234–257

EDGLEY, R. "Practical Reason," *Mind*, 74 (1965), 174–191

EDWARDS, R. B. "Agency without a Substantive Self," *Monist*, 49 (1965), 273–289

EHMAN, ROBERT R. "Causality and Agency," *Ratio*, 9 (1967), 140–154

ELLIS, BRIAN. See Austin, 1951–52

– See Braithwaite, R. B., 1955–56

EVANS, J. L. "Knowledge and Behaviour," *Proc. Arist. Soc.*, 54 (1953–54), 27–48

–"Error and the Will," *Philosophy*, 38 (1963), 136–148

EWING, A. C. See Warnock and Ewing, 1957

EWING, A. C., O. S. FRANKS, and J. MACMURRAY. "Symposium: What is Action?" *Proc. Arist. Soc. Supp.*, 17 (1938), 69–120

FAIN, HASKELL. "Prediction and Constraint," *Mind*, 67 (1958), 366–378

–"Hart and Honoré on Causation in the Law," *Inquiry*, 9 (1966), 322–338

FALK, W. D. See Barnes, Falk, and Duncan-Jones, 1945

–" 'Ought' and Motivation," *Proc. Arist. Soc.*, 48 (1947–48), 111–138

–"Action-Guiding Reasons," *J. Phil.*, 60 (1963), 702–718

FARRELL, B. A., MARGARET BRAITHWAITE, and C. A. MACE. "Symposium: Causal Laws in Psychology," *Proc. Arist. Soc. Supp.*, 23 (1949), 30–68

FARRELL, B. A., P. M. TURQUET, and J. O. WISDOM. "Symposium: The Criteria for a Psychoanalytic Interpretation," *Proc. Arist. Soc. Supp.*, 36 (1962), 77–144

FARRER, AUSTIN. *The Freedom of the Will*. London: Adams and Charles Block, 1958

FEINBERG, JOEL. "Problematic Responsibility in Law and Morals," *Phil. Rev.*, 71 (1962), 340–351

– (a) "On Being 'Morally Speaking a Murderer,' " *J. Phil.*, 61 (1964), 158–171

– (b) "Causing Voluntary Actions" [with comments by Keith Donnellan and Keith Lehrer, and rejoinders], in *Metaphysics and Explanation*, Oberlin Colloquium in Philosophy, edited by W. H. Capitan and D. D. Merrill. Pittsburgh: University of Pittsburgh Press, 1964. Pp. 29–61

–"Action and Responsibility," in *Philosophy in America*, edited by Max Black. Ithaca, NY: Cornell University Press, 1965. Pp. 135–160

FINDLAY, J. N. "Linguistic Approach to Psycho-Physics," *Proc. Arist. Soc.*, 50 (1949–50), 43–64

–"The Justification of Attitudes," *Mind*, 63 (1954), 145–161

– *Values and Intentions*. London: George Allen & Unwin, 1961

FINGARETTE, HERBERT. " 'Unconscious Behavior' and Allied Concepts: A New Approach to Their Empirical Interpretation," *J. Phil.*, 47 (1950), 509–520

–"Psychoanalytic Perspectives on Moral Guilt and Responsibility," *Phil. Phenomenol. Res.*, 16 (1955–56), 18–36

FISK, MILTON. "Causation and Action," *Rev. Metaph.*, 19 (1965–66), 235–247

–"A Defense of the Principle of Event Causality," *Brit. J. Phil. Sci.*, 18 (1967), 89–108

FITZGERALD, P. J. "Voluntary and Involuntary Acts," in *Oxford Essays in Jurisprudence*, edited by A. G. Guest. Oxford: Clarendon Press, 1961. Pp. 1–28

–"Acting and Refraining," *Analysis*, 27 (1967), 133–139

FLEMING, B. N. "On Intention," *Phil. Rev.*, 73 (1964), 301–320

FLEW, ANTHONY. "Psycho-Analytic Explanation," *Analysis*, 10 (1949–50), 8–15

–"Motives and The Unconscious," *Minnesota Studies in the Philosophy of Science*, I, edited by Herbert Feigl and Michael Scriven. Minneapolis: University of Minnesota Press, 1956. Pp. 155–173

–"Determinism and Rational Behaviour," *Mind*, 68 (1959), 377–382

FODOR, JERRY A. "Explanations in Psychology," *Philosophy in America*, edited by Max Black. Ithaca, NY: Cornell University Press, 1965. Pp. 161–179

FOOT, PHILLIPA. "Free Will as Involving Determinism," *Phil. Rev.*, 66 (1957), 439–450

–"Hart and Honoré: Causation in the Law," *Phil. Rev.*, 72 (1963), 505–515

FORGUSON, L. W. "La Philosophie de L'Action de J. L. Austin," *Arch. Phil.*, 30 (1967), 36–60

FOSTER, J. A. "Psychophysical Causal Relations," *Amer. Phil. Quart.*, 5 (1968), 64–70

FRANK, JEROME. *Fate and Freedom.* New York: Simon and Schuster, 1945

FRANKENA, WILLIAM K. (a) "J. D. Wild on Responsibility," *Phil. Phenomenol. Res.*, 27 (1966–67), 90–96

– (b) "Reply to Professor Wild," *Phil. Phenomenol. Res.*, 27 (1966–67), 103

FRANKLIN, R. L. "Dissolving the Problem of Freewill," *Austl. J. Phil.*, 39 (1961), 111–123

–"Moral Libertarianism," *Phil. Quart.*, 12 (1962), 24–35

– *Freewill and Determinism.* London: Routledge & Kegan Paul, 1968

FRANKS, O. S. See Ewing, Franks, and Macmurray, 1938

GAHRINGER, ROBERT E. "The Foundation of Necessity in Practical Reason," *Int. Phil. Quart.*, 2 (1962), 25–49

GALLAGHER, KENNETH T. "On Choosing to Choose," *Mind*, 73 (1964), 480–495

GALLIE, IAN. "Intelligence and Intelligent Conduct," *Proc. Arist. Soc.*, 48 (1947–48), 187–204

GALLIE, W. B., W. J. H. SPROTT, and C. A. MACE. "Symposium: Does Psychology Study Mental Acts or Dispositions?" *Proc. Arist. Soc. Supp.*, 21 (1947), 134–174

GALLOP, DAVID. "On Being Determined," *Mind*, 71 (1962), 181–196

–"Ayers on 'Could' and 'Could Have,' " *Phil. Quart.*, 17 (1967), 255–256

GARDINER, PATRICK. *The Nature of Historical Explanation.* London: Oxford University Press, 1952

–, ed. *Theories of History.* Glencoe, Ill.: The Free Press, 1959

GARNETT, A. C. "Responsibility and Self-Determination," *J. Phil.*, 47 (1950), 526–530

–"Freedom and Creativity," *Proc. and Addresses of the APA*, 34 (1960–61), 25–39

GARVIN, LUCIUS. "Obligation and Moral Agency," *Ethics*, 58 (1947–48), 188–194

GASKINGS, DOUGLAS. See Austin, 1951–52

GAUTHIER, DAVID P. *Practical Reasoning.* Oxford: Clarendon Press, 1963

–"How Decisions Are Caused," *J. Phil.*, 64 (1967), 147–151

GEACH, P. T. *Mental Acts.* New York: Humanities Press, 1957

–"Ascriptivism," *Phil. Rev.*, 69 (1960), 221–225

–"Dr. Kenny on Practical Inference," *Analysis*, 26 (1965–66), 76–79

GEAN, W. D. "Reasons and Causes," *Rev. Metaph.*, 19 (1965–66), 667–688

GEORGE, ROLF A. "Acting upon a Proposition," *Analysis*, 23 (1962–63), 116–118

GERT, BERNARD. See Duggan and Gert, 1967

GIBSON, A. BOYCE. "Reason in Practice," *Austl. J. Phil.*, 45 (1967), 1–14

GINET, CARL. "Can the Will Be Caused?" *Phil. Rev.*, 71 (1962), 340–351

–"Might We Have No Choice?" in Lehrer, 1966, pp. 88–104

GLASGOW, W. D. "On Choosing," *Analysis*, 17 (1956–57), 135–139

–"The Concept of Choosing," *Analysis*, 20 (1959–60), 63–67

GOLDBERG, BRUCE. "Can a Desire Be a Cause?" *Analysis*, 25 (1964–65), 70–72

GOLDBERG, BRUCE and H. HEIDELBERGER. "Mr. Lehrer on the Constitution of Cans," *Analysis*, 21 (1960–61), 96

GOLDING, M. P. "Causation in the Law," *J. Phil.*, 59 (1962), 85–95

GOLDMAN, ALVIN I. "Predictions and Books of Life," *Amer. Phil. Quart.*, 5 (1968), 135–151

GORDON, L. M. "The Range of Application of 'Voluntary,' 'Not Voluntary' and 'Involuntary,' " *Analysis*, 26 (1965–66), 149–152

GOSLING, JUSTIN. "Mental Causes and Fear," *Mind*, 71 (1962), 289–306

–"Emotion and Object," *Phil. Rev.*, 74 (1965), 486–503

GOULD, JAMES A. "A Note on Willing the First Time," *Thomist*, 32 (1968), 424–429

GRANT, C. K. "Freewill: A Reply to Professor Campbell," *Mind*, 61 (1952), 381–385

– *Belief and Action.* Durham: University of Durham, 1960

GRAVE, S. A. "Too Good a Reason to Be a Reason," *Analysis,* 20 (1959–60), 37–41

GRIFFITHS, A. P. "Acting with Reason," *Phil. Quart.,* 8 (1958), 289–299

GRUNER, ROLF. (a) "Plurality of Causes," *Philosophy,* 42 (1967), 367–374

– (b) "Understanding the Social Sciences and History," *Inquiry,* 10 (1967), 151–163

GUSTAFSON, DON F. "Voluntary and Involuntary," *Phil. Phenomenol. Res.,* 23 (1962–63), 493–501

–, ed. (a) *Essays in Philosophical Psychology.* New York: Doubleday, 1964

– (b) "Explanation in Psychology," *Mind,* 73 (1964), 280–281

–"Momentary Intentions," *Mind,* 77 (1968), 1–13

HAKSAR, VINIT and C. H. WHITELEY, "Symposium: Responsibility," *Proc. Arist. Soc. Supp.,* 40 (1966), 187–234

HALVERSON, W. H. "The Bogy of Chance: A Reply to Professor Smart," *Mind,* 73 (1964), 567–570

HAMBURGH, C. H. "Arguments, Actions and Some Intellectuals," *Ethics,* 73 (1962–63), 287–292

HAMLYN, D. W. "Behaviour," *Philosophy,* 28 (1953), 132–145

HAMLYN, D. W. and J. J. C. SMART. "Symposium: Causality and Human Behaviour," *Proc. Arist. Soc. Supp.,* 38 (1964), 125–148

HAMPSHIRE, STUART. "Critical Notice of *The Concept of Mind* by Gilbert Ryle," *Mind,* 59 (1950), 237–255

– *Thought and Action.* London: Chatto and Windus, 1959

– *Feeling and Expression.* London: H. K. Lewis, 1960

–"Reply to Walsh on *Thought and Action,*" *J. Phil.,* 60 (1963), 410–424

– *Freedom of the Individual.* New York: Harper and Row, 1965

HAMPSHIRE, STUART and H. L. A. HART. "Decision, Intention and Certainty," *Mind,* 67 (1958), 1–12

HANDY, ROLLO. "Determinism, Responsibility and the Social Setting," *Phil. Phenomenol. Res.,* 20 (1959–60), 469–476

HARDIE, W. F. R. "Mr. Toulmin on the Explanation of Human Conduct," *Analysis,* 11 (1950–51), 1–8

-"My Own Free Will," *Philosophy*, 32 (1957), 21–38

HARE, RICHARD M. *The Language of Morals*. Oxford: Clarendon Press, 1952

-"Critical Study of M. G. Singer's *Generalization in Ethics*," *Phil. Quart.*, 12 (1962), 351–355

- *Freedom and Reason*. Oxford: Oxford University Press, 1963

HART, H. L. A. "The Ascription of Responsibility and Rights," *Proc. Arist. Soc.*, 49 (1948–49), 171–194

- See Hampshire and Hart, 1958

HART, H. L. A. and A. M. HONORÉ. *Causation in the Law*. Oxford: Clarendon Press, 1959

HARTNACK, JUSTUS. "Free Will and Decision," *Mind*, 62 (1953), 367–374

-"Freedom and Equality," *Danish Yearbook of Philosophy*, 3 (1966), 7–14

-"The Concept of Act and Behavior," *Man and World*, 1 (1968), 267–277

HARTSHORNE, CHARLES. "Freedom Requires Indeterminism and Universal Causality," *J. Phil.*, 55 (1958), 793–811

-"The Meaning of 'Is Going To Be,'" *Mind*, 74 (1965), 46–58

HEATH, P. L. See Passmore and Heath, 1955

HEIDELBERGER, H. See Goldberg and Heidelberger, 1960–61

HEMPEL, CARL G. "The Function of General Laws in History," *J. Phil.*, 39 (1942), 35–48

-"Rational Action," *Proc. and Addresses of the APA*, 35 (1961–62), 5–23

- (a) "Deductive-Nomological vs. Statistical Explanation," *Minnesota Studies in the Philosophy of Science*, III, edited by Herbert Feigl and Grover Maxwell. Minneapolis: University of Minnesota Press, 1962. Pp. 98–169

- (b) "Explanation in Science and in History," *Frontiers of Science and Philosophy*, edited by Robert G. Colodny. Pittsburgh: University of Pittsburgh Press, 1962. Pp. 7–33

HEMPEL, CARL G. and PAUL OPPENHEIM. "The Logic of Explanation," *Philosophy of Science*, 15 (1948), 135–175

HENDERSON, G. P. "Predictability in Human Affairs," in Royal Institute of Philosophy, 1968, pp. 1–19

HENSON, R. G. "Responsibility for Character and Responsibility for Conduct," *Austl. J. Phil.*, 43 (1965), 311–320

HERBST, P. "Freedom and Prediction," *Mind*, 66 (1957), 1–27

HINTZ, H. W. "Causation, Will and Creativity," *J. Phil.*, 55 (1958), 514–520

HOLBOROW, L. C. "Wittgenstein's Kind of Behaviourism," *Phil. Quart.*, 17 (1967), 345–357

HONORÉ, A. M. See Hart and Honoré, 1959

–"Can and Can't," *Mind*, 73 (1964), 463–479

HOOK, SIDNEY, ed. *Determinism and Freedom in the Age of Modern Science*. New York: New York University Press, 1958

–, ed. *Psychoanalysis, Scientific Method and Philosophy*. New York: New York University Press, 1959

–, ed. *Dimensions of Mind*. New York: New York University Press, 1960

HORSBURGH, H. J. N. "Freedom and Real Will Theories," *Austl. J. Phil.*, 34 (1956), 92–105

HOSPERS, JOHN. "Meaning and Free Will," *Phil. Phenomenol. Res.*, 10 (1949–50), 307–330

HUBY, PAMELA. "The First Discovery of the Freewill Problem," *Philosophy*, 42 (1967), 353–362

IMLAY, R. A. "Do I Ever Directly Raise My Arm?" *Philosophy*, 42 (1967), 119–127

JACK, HENRY. "Genuine Choice and Blame," *Dialogue*, 4 (1965–66), 72–81

JAGER, RONALD. "Describing Acts Owing to Ignorance," *Analysis*, 27 (1967), 163–167

JARVIS, JUDITH. "Practical Reasoning," *Phil. Quart.*, 12 (1962), 316–328

JEFFREY, R. C. "Ethics and the Logic of Decision," *J. Phil.*, 62 (1965), 528–539

JENKINS, J. J. "Motive and Intention," *Phil. Quart.*, 15 (1965), 155–164

–"Dr. Peter's Motives," *Mind*, 75 (1966), 248–254

KADING, DANIEL. "Mr. Mothershead's Two Concepts of Freedom," *J. Phil.*, 50 (1953), 664–668

–"Moral Action, Ignorance of Fact, and Inability," *Phil. Phenomenol. Res.*, 25 (1964–65), 333–355

KADISH, M. R. "Evidence and Decision," *J. Phil.*, 48 (1951), 229–242

KANBEMBO, DANIEL. "Essai d'une Ontologie de l'Agir," *Rev. Phil. Louvain*, 65 (1967), 356–387

KASHOP, PAUL. "Can a Man Act upon a Proposition Which He Believes to Be False?" *Analysis*, 22 (1961–62), 31–36

KATZ, JOSEPH. "Desiring Reason," *J. Phil.*, 53 (1956), 835–843

KAUFMAN, A. S. "Moral Responsibility and the Use of 'Could Have,' " *Phil. Quart.*, 12 (1962), 120–128

–"Ability," *J. Phil.*, 60 (1963), 537–551

–"Practical Decision," *Mind*, 75 (1966), 25–44

KELSEN, HANS. "Causality and Imputation," *Ethics*, 61 (1950–51), 1–11

KEMP, DAVID. "Do We Learn How to Behave Morally?" *Mind*, 67 (1958), 408

KENNER, LIONEL. "Causality, Determinism and Freedom of the Will," *Philosophy*, 39 (1964), 233–248

KENNY, ANTHONY J. *Action, Emotion and Will*. London: Routledge & Kegan Paul, 1963

–"Practical Inference," *Analysis*, 26 (1965–66), 65–75

– (a) "Intention and Purpose," *J. Phil.*, 63 (1966), 642–651

– (b) "The Practical Syllogism and Incontinence," *Phronesis*, 11 (1966), 163–184

KHATCHADOURIAN, HAIG. "What Is Rationality?" *Theoria*, 24 (1958), 172–187

KIM, JAEGWON. See Brandt and Kim, 1963

KINBERG, OLAF. "Motive, Choice, Will," *Theoria*, 14 (1948), 209–237

KING, H. R. "Professor Ryle and *The Concept of Mind*," *J. Phil.* 48 (1951), 280–296

KING-FARLOW, JOHN. "Mr. Bradley and the Libertarians," *Austl. J. Phil.*, 37 (1959), 234–238

KNOX, JOHN, JR. "Blanchard on Causation and Necessity," *Rev. Metaph.*, 20 (1966–67), 518–532

KOLENDA, KONSTANTIN. "Unconscious Motives and Human Actions," *Inquiry*, 7 (1964), 1–12

KOLNAI, AUREL. "Agency and Freedom," in Royal Institute of Philosophy, 1968, pp. 20–46

KÖRNER, STEPHEN. "Science and Moral Responsibility," *Mind*, 73 (1964), 161–172

KOTARBINSKI, T. "The Concept of Action," *J. Phil.*, 57 (1960), 215–222

–"Practical Error," *Danish Yearbook of Philosophy*, 1 (1964), 65–71

– *Praxiology*, translated by Olgierd Wojtasiewicz. Oxford: Pergamon Press, 1965

LACEY, A. R. "Freewill and Responsibility," *Proc. Arist. Soc.*, 58 (1957–58), 15–32

LADD, JOHN. "Free Will and Voluntary Action," *Phil. Phenomenol. Res.*, 12 (1951–52), 392–405

–"Ethics and Explanation," *J. Phil.*, 49 (1952), 499–504

–"The Ethical Dimension of the Concept of Action," *J. Phil.*, 62 (1965), 633–645

LANDESMAN, CHARLES. "Mental Events," *Phil. Phenomenol. Res.*, 23 (1962–63), 307–317

–"The New Dualism in the Philosophy of Mind," *Rev. Metaph.*, 19 (1965), 329–345

– See Care and Landesman, 1968

LAWRENCE, NATHANIEL. "Causality, Will and Time," *Rev. Metaph.*, 9 (1955–56), 14–26

–"Causality: Causes as Classes," *Rev. Metaph.*, 12 (1958–59), 161–185

LEDDEN, J. E. "Contextual and Intrinsic Freedom," *J. Phil.*, 46 (1949), 702–708

LEHRER, KEITH. "Ifs, Cans and Causes," *Analysis*, 20 (1959–60), 122–124

–"Can We Know that We Have Free Will by Introspection?" *J. Phil.*, 57 (1960), 145–157

–"Cans and Conditionals: a Rejoinder," *Analysis*, 22 (1961–62), 23–24

–"Decisions and Causes," *Phil. Rev.*, 72 (1963), 224–227

–" 'Could' and Determinism," *Analysis*, 24 (1963–64), 159–160

– (a) "Doing the Impossible," *Austl. J. Phil.*, 42 (1964), 86–97

– (b) "Doing the Impossible: a Second Try," *Austl. J. Phil.*, 42 (1964), 249–251

– (c) See Feinberg, 1964

–, ed. *Freedom and Determinism*. New York: Random House, 1966

– See Alston, 1967

LEHRER, KEITH, R. ROELOFS, and M. SWAIN. "Reasons and Evidence, an Unsolved Problem," *Ratio*, 9 (1967), 38–48

LEMMON, E. J. See Davidson, 1967

LEMOS, R. M. "Determinism, Indeterminism, and Freedom," *J. Phil.*, 56 (1959), 959–960

LOCKE, DON. "Ifs and Cans Revisited," *Philosophy*, 37 (1962), 245–256

LONG, THOMAS A. "Hampshire on Animals and Intentions," *Mind*, 72 (1963), 414–416

LOUCH, A. R. "Anthropology and Moral Explanation," *Monist*, 47 (1962–63), 610–624

–"On Misunderstanding Mr. Winch," *Inquiry*, 8 (1965), 212–216

– *Explanation and Human Action*. Berkeley: University of California Press, 1966

LYON, ARDON. "Causality," *Brit. J. Phil. Sci.*, 18 (1967), 1–20

MABBOTT, J. D. "Reason and Desire," *Philosophy*, 28 (1953), 113–123

MCADAM, JAMES I. "Choosing Flippantly or Non-rational Choice," *Analysis*, 25 (1964–65), 132–136

MACCALLUM, GERALD C., JR. "Negative and Positive Freedom," *Phil. Rev.*, 76 (1967), 312–334

MCCLOSKEY, H. J. "Nowell-Smith's *Ethics*," *Austl. J. Phil.*, 39 (1961), 251–275

–"Some Concepts of Cause," *Rev. Metaph.*, 17 (1963–64), 586–607

MCCORMICK, SUSANNE and IRVING THALBERG. "Trying," *Dialogue*, 6 (1967), 29–46

MCCRACKEN, D. J. See Peters, McCracken, and Urmson, 1952

MACDONALD, MARGARET, ed. *Philosophy and Analysis*. Oxford: Blackwell, 1954

MACE, C. A. See Gallie, Sprott, and Mace, 1947

– See Farrell, Braithwaite, and Mace, 1949

MACE, C. A. and R. S. PETERS. "Emotions and the Category of Passivity," *Proc. Arist. Soc.*, 62 (1961–62), 117–142

MCGUINESS, B. F. "I Know What I Want," *Proc. Arist. Soc.*, 57 (1956–57) 305–320

MACINTYRE, ALISDAIR. See Alexander and MacIntyre, 1955

–"Determinism," *Mind*, 66 (1957), 28–41

– *The Unconscious: A Conceptual Analysis*. New York: Humanities Press, 1958

–"Hume on 'Is' and 'Ought,' " *Phil. Rev.*, 68 (1959)

–"A Mistake about Causality in Social Science," in *Philosophy, Politics, and Society*, Second Series, edited by Peter Laslett and W. G. Runciman. Oxford: Blackwell, 1962. Pp. 48–70

– (a) "Imperatives, Reasons for Action, and Morals," *J. Phil.*, 62 (1965), 513–524

– (b) "Pleasure as a Reason for Action," *Monist*, 49 (1965), 215–233

–"The Antecedents of Action," in *British Analytical Philosophy*, edited by Bernard Williams and Alan Montefiore. London: Routledge & Kegan Paul, 1966. Pp. 205–225

MACINTYRE, ALISDAIR and P. H. NOWELL-SMITH. "Symposium: Purpose and Intelligent Action," *Proc. Arist. Soc. Supp.*, 34 (1960), 79–112

MACKAY, D. M. "Brain and Will," *The Listener*, 57 (1957), 745–746, 788–789

–"On the Logical Indeterminacy of a Free Choice," *Mind*, 69 (1960), 31–40

–"Logical Indeterminacy and Freewill," *Analysis*, 21 (1960–61), 82–83

MCKEON, RICHARD. "Philosophy and Action," *Ethics*, 62 (1951–52), 79–100

– *Thought, Action and Passion*. Chicago: University of Chicago Press, 1954

–"Mankind: The Relation of Reason to Action," *Ethics*, 74 (1963–64), 174–185

MACKIE, J. L. "Responsibility and Language," *Austl. J. Phil.*, 33 (1955), 143–159

–"Causes and Conditions," *Amer. Phil. Quart.*, 2 (1965), 245–264

MACKLIN, RUTH. "Actions, Consequences and Ethical Theory," *J. Value Inq.*, 1 (1967), 72–80

MCLAUGHLIN, R. N. "Human Action," *Austl. J. Phil.*, 45 (1967), 141–158

MACMURRAY, J. See Ewing, Franks, and Macmurray, 1938

– *The Self as Agent*. New York: Humanities Press, 1957

MADDEN, E. H. "Psychoanalysis and Moral Judgeability," *Phil. Phenomenol. Res.*, 18 (1957–58), 68–79

MADELL, GEOFFREY. "Action and Causal Explanation," *Mind*, 76 (1967), 34–48

MAKEPEACE, PETER. "Fatalism and Ability," *Analysis*, 23 (1962–63), 27–29

MALCOLM, NORMAN. "Explaining Behaviour," *Phil. Rev.*, 76 (1967), 97–104

–"The Conceivability of Mechanism," *Phil. Rev.*, 77 (1968), 45–72

MANDELBAUM, MAURICE. "Determinism and Moral Responsibility," *Ethics*, 70 (1959–60), 204–219

MANNISON, DONALD S. "My Motive and Its Reasons," *Mind*, 73 (1964), 423–429

MARGOLIS, JOSEPH. "Actions and Ways of Failing," *Inquiry*, 3 (1960), 89–101

MARTIN, MICHAEL. "Winch on Philosophy, Social Science and Explanation," *Phil. Forum*, 23 (1965–66) 29–41

MASTERMAN, MARGARET. "The Psychology of Levels of Will," *Proc. Arist. Soc.*, 48 (1947–48), 75–110

– See Farrell, Braithwaite, and Mace 1949

MATSON, W. I. "On the Irrelevance of Free-Will to Moral Responsibility, and the Vacuity of the Latter," *Mind*, 65 (1956), 489–497

MATTHEWS, G. M. See Austin, 1951–52

–"Weakness of Will," *Mind*, 75 (1966), 405–419

MATTHEWS, GARETH B. and S. MARC COHEN. "Wants and Lacks," *J. Phil.*, 64 (1967), 455–456

MAYO, BERNARD. "Commitments and Reasons," *Mind*, 64 (1955), 342–360

–"A Logical Limitation on Determinism." *Philosophy*, 33 (1958), 50–55

–"The Moral Agent," in Royal Institute of Philosophy, 1968, pp. 47–63

MAYS, W. "Determinism and Free Will in Whitehead," *Phil.
Phenomenol. Res.*, 15 (1954–55), 523–534

MEILAND, J. W. (a) "Are There Unintentional Actions?"
Phil. Rev., 72 (1963), 377–381

– (b) "Motives and Ends," *Phil. Quart.*, 13 (1963), 64–71

MELDEN, A. I. "Action," *Phil. Rev.*, 65 (1956), 523–541

–"My Kinaesthetic Sensations Advise Me ...," *Analysis*, 18
(1957), 43–48

– *Rights and Right Conduct*. Oxford: Blackwell, 1959

–"Willing," *Phil. Rev.*, 69 (1960), 475–484

– *Free Action*. London: Routledge & Kegan Paul, 1961

–"Reasons for Action and Matters of Fact," *Proc. and
Addresses of the APA*, 35 (1961–62), 45–60

–"Philosophy and the Understanding of Human Fact," in
Stroll, 1967, pp. 229–249

MELLOR, D. H. "Two Fallacies in Charles Taylor's Explanation
of Behaviour," *Mind*, 77 (1968), 124–126

MELLOR, W. W. "Knowing, Believing and Behaving," *Mind*, 76
(1967), 327–345

MICHEKAKIS, E. M. *Aristotle's Theory of Practical Principles*.
Athens: Cleisiounis Press, 1961

MISCHEL, THEODORE. "Psychology and Explanations of Human
Behaviour," *Phil. Phenomenol. Res.*, 23 (1962–63), 578–594

–"Concerning Rational Behaviour and Psychoanalytic
Explanation," *Mind*, 74 (1965), 71–78

–"Pragmatic Aspects of Explanation," *Philosophy of Science*,
33 (1966), 40–60

–, ed. *Human Action*. New York: Academic Press Inc., 1969

MISH'ALANI, JAMES K. "Can Right Acts Be Voluntary?"
Analysis, 20 (1959–60), 67–72

MONTAGUE, RICHARD. "Logical Necessity, Physical Necessity,
Ethics and Quantifiers," *Inquiry*, 3 (1960), 259–269

MONTAGUE, ROGER. "Mr. Bradley on the Future," *Mind*, 69
(1960), 550–554

–"Choosing Chisels and Deciding to Get Up," *Mind*, 76
(1967), 428–429

MONTEFIORE, ALAN. "Determinism and Causal Order," *Proc.
Arist. Soc.*, 58 (1957–58), 125–142

MOORE, ASHER. "Emotivism and Intentionality," *Ethics*, 71
(1960–61), 175–187

MORGENBESSER, S. See Danto and Morgenbesser, 1957
–"Symposium: Human Action (Introductory Remarks),"
J. Phil., 60 (1963), 365–367

MORGENBESSER, S. and J. WALSH, eds. *Free Will*. Englewood
Cliffs, NJ: Prentice-Hall, 1962

MOSER, SHIA. "Decisions, Commands and Moral Judgments,"
Phil. Phenomenol. Res., 18 (1957–58), 471–488

MOTHERSHEAD, J. L., JR. "Some Reflections on the Meanings of
Freedom," *J. Phil.*, 49 (1952), 667–672

MOTHERSILL, MARY. "Agents, Critics, and Philosophers," *Mind*,
69 (1960), 433–446
–"Professor Prior and Jonathan Edwards," *Rev. Metaph.*, 16
(1962–63), 366–373

MULLANE, HARVEY. "Unconscious Emotion," *Theoria*, 31 (1965),
181–190
–"Moral Responsibility for Dreams," *Dialogue*, 4 (1965–66),
224–229
–"Dreaming as an Action," *Dialogue*, 5 (1966–67), 239–242

MUNK, A. W. "The Self as Agent and Spectator," *Monist*, 49
(1965), 262–272

MUNN, ALLAN M. *Free Will and Determinism*. Toronto: University
of Toronto Press, 1960

MURPHY, ARTHUR E. "Jonathan Edwards on Free Will and Moral
Agency," *Phil. Rev.*, 68 (1959), 181–202
– *The Theory of Practical Reasoning*. LaSalle: Open Court, 1964

MYERS, FRANCIS M. "Three Types of Freedom," *Inquiry*, 10
(1967), 337–350

MYERS, GERALD E. "Feeling into Words," *J. Phil.*, 60 (1963),
801–810
–"Motives and Wants," *Mind*, 73 (1964), 173–185

NAKHNIKIAN, GEORGE. See Castañeda and Nakhnikian, 1965

NOWELL-SMITH, P. H. "Freewill and Moral Responsibility,"
Mind, 57 (1948), 45–61
– (a) "Determinists and Libertarians," *Mind*, 63 (1954),
317–337
– (b) *Ethics*. Harmondsworth: Penguin Books, 1954

–"Choosing, Deciding and Doing," *Analysis*, 18 (1957–58), 63–69
– (a) "Ifs and Cans," *Theoria*, 26 (1960), 85–101
– (b) See MacIntyre and Nowell-Smith, 1960

O'CONNOR, D. J. "Is There a Problem about Free Will?" *Proc. Arist. Soc.*, 49 (1948–49), 33–46
–"Possibility and Choice," *Prod. Arist. Soc. Supp.*, 34 (1960), 1–24
–"How Decisions Are Predicted," *J. Phil.*, 64 (1967), 429–430
OFSTAD, HARALD. "Can We Produce Decisions?" *J. Phil.*, 56 (1959), 89–94
– *An Inquiry into the Freedom of Decision.* London: George Allan & Unwin, 1961
–"Recent Work on the Free-Will Problem," *Amer. Phil. Quart.*, 4 (1967), 179–207
OLBRECHTS-TYTECA, L. See Perelman and Olbrechts-Tyteca, 1950–51
OLDENQUIST, ANDREW. "Causes, Predictions and Decisions," *Analysis*, 24 (1963–64), 55–58
OLSHEWSKY, T. M. "A Third Dogma of Empiricism," *Monist*, 49 (1965), 304–318
OPPENHEIM, F. E. "Rational Choice," *J. Phil.*, 50 (1953), 341–350
– *Dimensions of Freedom: An Analysis.* New York: St. Martin's Press, 1961
OPPENHEIM, PAUL. See Hempel and Oppenheim, 1948
OSBORN, JANE M. "Austin's Non-Conditional Ifs," *J. Phil.*, 62 (1965), 711–715
O'SHAUGHNESSY, BRIAN. "The Limits of the Will," *Phil. Rev.*, 65 (1956), 443–490
–"Observation and the Will," *J. Phil.*, 60 (1963), 367–392

PAHUUS, MOGENS. "On Determinism and the Nature of Persons," *Danish Yearbook of Philosophy*, 3 (1966), 82–88
PAP, ARTHUR. "Determinism and Moral Responsibility," *J. Phil.*, 43 (1946), 318–327
PAPANOUTOS, E. P. "Freedom and Causality," *Philosophy*, 34 (1959), 193–203

PARSONS, H. L. "Reason and Affect: Some of Their Relations and Functions," *J. Phil.*, 55 (1958), 221–230

PASSMORE, J. A. and P. L. HEATH. "Symposium: 'Intentions,' " *Proc. Arist. Soc. Supp.*, 29 (1955), 131–165

PATTON, T. E. "Reasoning in Moral Matters," *J. Phil.*, 53 (1956), 523–531

PEARS, D. F., ed. *Freedom and the Will*. London: Macmillan, 1963

– *Predicting and Deciding*. London: Oxford University Press, 1964

–"Are Reasons for Actions Causes?" in Stroll, 1967, pp. 204–228

–"Desires as Causes of Actions," in Royal Institute of Philosophy, 1968, pp. 83–97

PERELMAN, C. "The Theoretical Relations of Thought and Action," *Inquiry*, 1 (1958), 130–136

–"Reply to Stanley H. Rosen," *Inquiry*, 2 (1959), 85–88

PERELMAN, C. and L. OLBRECHTS-TYTECA. "Act and Person in Argument," *Ethics*, 61 (1950–51), 251–269

PERKINS, MORELAND. (a) "Emotion and the Concept of Behavior," *Amer. Phil. Quart.*, 3 (1966), 291–298

– (b) "Emotion and Feeling," *Phil. Rev.*, 75 (1966), 139–160

PERRY, D. L. "Prediction, Explanation and Freedom," *Monist*, 49 (1965), 234–247

PERRY, R. C. "Professor Ayer's 'Freedom and Necessity,' " *Mind*, 70 (1961), 228–234

PETERS, RICHARD. "Cause, Cure and Motive," *Analysis*, 10 (1949–50), 103–109

–"Observationalism in Psychology," *Mind*, 60 (1951), 43–61

–"Motives and Motivation," *Philosophy*, 31 (1956), 117–130

– *The Concept of Motivation*. London: Routledge & Kegan Paul, 1958

– See Mace and Peters, 1961–62

PETERS, RICHARD, D. J. MCCRACKEN, and J. O. URMSON. "Symposium: Motives and Causes," *Proc. Arist. Soc. Supp.*, 26 (1952), 139–194

PHILLIPS, D. Z. and H. S. PRICE. "Remorse without Repudiation," *Analysis*, 28 (1967), 15–20

PIKE, NELSON. "Divine Omniscience and Voluntary Action,"
Phil. Rev., 74 (1965), 27–46

–"Of God and Freedom: A Rejoinder," *Phil. Rev.*, 75 (1966),
369–379

PITCHER, GEORGE. "Hart on Action and Responsibility," *Phil.
Rev.*, 69 (1960), 226–235

–"Necessitarianism," *Phil. Quart.*, 11 (1961), 201–212

–, ed. *Wittgenstein, The Philosophical Investigations.* Garden
City, NY: Doubleday, 1966

POPPER, KARL. *Conjectures and Refutations.* New York: Basic
Books, 1962

POWELL, BETTY. "Uncharacteristic Actions," *Mind*, 68 (1959),
492–509

– *Knowledge of Actions.* London: George Allen & Unwin, 1967

PRICE, H. H. "Belief and Will," *Proc. Arist. Soc. Supp.*, 28
(1954), 1–26

PRICE, H. S. See Phillips and Price, 1967

PRICHARD, H. A. *Moral Obligation.* Oxford: Clarendon Press,
1949

PRIOR, A. N. "Limited Indeterminism," *Rev. Metaph.*, 16
(1962–63), 55–61

PRIOR, A. N. and D. D. RAPHAEL. "Symposium: The Consequences
of Actions," *Proc. Arist. Soc. Supp.*, 30 (1956), 91–119

QUINE, W. V. O. *Word and Object.* Cambridge, Mass.: The
MIT Press, 1960

RAAB, FRANCIS V. "Free Will and the Ambiguity of 'Could,' "
Phil. Rev., 64 (1955), 60–77

RADCLIFF, PETER. "Beliefs, Attitudes and Actions," *Dialogue*, 4
(1965–66), 456–464

RANKIN, K. W. "Doer and Doing," *Mind*, 69 (1960), 361–371

– *Choice and Chance: A Libertarian Analysis.* Oxford: Blackwell,
1961

–"Wittgenstein on Meaning, Understanding, and Intending,"
Amer. Phil. Quart., 3 (1966), 1–13

RANKIN, NANI L. "The Unmoved Agent and the Ground of
Responsibility," *J. Phil.*, 64 (1967), 403–408

RAPHAEL, D. D. See Prior and Raphael, 1956

RAPOPORT, ANATOL. *Fights, Games, and Debates.* Ann Arbor: University of Michigan Press, 1960

RAUP, R. B. "Method in Judgments of Practice," *J. Phil.*, 46 (1949), 806–817

RAWLS, JOHN. "Two Concepts of Rules," *Phil. Rev.*, 64 (1955), 3–32

RAYFIELD, DAVID. "Action," *Noûs*, 2 (1968), 131–145

RESCHER, NICHOLAS. See Braithwaite, R. B., 1955–56

–"Practical Reasoning and Values," *Phil. Quart.*, 16 (1966), 121–136

– (a) "Aspects of Action," in Rescher 1967b, pp. 215–219

–, ed. (b) *The Logic of Decision and Action.* Pittsburgh: University of Pittsburgh Press, 1967

– (c) "Values and the Explanation of Behavior," *Phil. Quart.*, 17 (1967), 130–136

RIEFF, PHILIP. "History, Psychoanalysis and the Social Sciences," *Ethics*, 63 (1952–53), 107–120

–"Freudian Ethics and the Idea of Reason," *Ethics*, 67 (1956–57), 169–183

RIKER, W. H. "Events and Situations," *J. Phil.*, 54 (1957), 57–70

–"Causes of Events," *J. Phil.*, 55 (1958), 281–291

RITCHIE, A. M. "Agent and Act in Theory of Mind," *Proc. Arist. Soc.*, 52 (1951–52), 1–22

ROBINSON, PETER. "Speculative and Practical," *Heythrop J.*, 9 (1968), 37–49

ROBISON, J. See von Wright, 1967

ROELOFS, R. See Lehrer, Roelofs, and Swain, 1967

ROLSTON, HOWARD L. "Kinaesthetic Sensations Revisited," *J. Phil.*, 62 (1965), 96–100

RORETZ, KARL. "Modern Physics and the Freedom of the Will," *J. Phil.*, 55 (1958), 70–73

RORTY, A. O. "Wants and Justifications," *J. Phil.*, 63 (1966), 765–772

RORTY, RICHARD. "Mind-Body Identity, Privacy, and Categories," *Rev. Metaph.*, 19 (1965), 24–54

ROSEN, S. H. "Thought and Action," *Inquiry*, 2 (1959), 65–84

ROWE, WILLIAM L. "Augustine on Foreknowledge and Free Will," *Rev. Metaph.*, 18 (1964–65), 356–363

ROXBEE COX, J. W. "Can I Know Beforehand What I Am Going to Decide?" *Phil. Rev.*, 72 (1963), 88–92

ROYAL INSTITUTE OF PHILOSOPHY. *The Human Agent* (Royal Institute of Philosophy Lectures Volume I, 1966–67). London: Macmillan, 1968

RUYER, R. "Les Observables et les Participables," *Rev. Phil. Fr.*, 156 (1966), 419–450

RYAN, ALAN. "Freedom," *Philosophy*, 40 (1965), 93–112

RYLE, GILBERT. "Knowing How and Knowing That," *Proc. Arist. Soc.*, 46 (1945–46), 1–16

- *The Concept of Mind*. London: Hutchinson's University Library, 1949

SACHS, DAVID. "A Few Morals about Acts," *Phil. Rev.*, 75 (1966), 91–98

SAUNDERS, J. T. (a) "Fatalism and Linguistic Reform," *Analysis*, 23 (1962–63), 30–31

- (b) "Professor Taylor on Fatalism," *Analysis*, 23 (1962–63), 1–2

-"Fatalism and the Logic of 'Ability,' " *Analysis*, 24 (1963–64), 24

-"Fatalism and Ordinary Language," *J. Phil.*, 62 (1965), 211–222

-"Of God and Freedom," *Phil. Rev.*, 75 (1966), 219–225

SCARROW, DAVID S. "On an Analysis of 'Could Have,' " *Analysis*, 23 (1962–63), 118–120

-"Hare's Account of Moral Reasoning," *Ethics*, 76 (1965–66), 137–141

SCHEER, RICHARD K. "Predictions of Events," *Phil. Quart.*, 17 (1967), 257–261

SCHNEEWIND, J. B. "Comments on Prior's Paper," *Rev. Metaph.*, 16 (1962–63), 374–379

SCHON, DONALD. "Rationality in Retrospective and Prospective Deliberation," *Phil. Phenomenol. Res.*, 20 (1959–60), 477–486

SCHUETZ, A. "Choosing among Projects of Action," *Phil. Phenomenol. Res.*, 12 (1951–52), 161–184

SCOTT, K. J. "Conditioning and Freedom," *Austl. J. Phil.*, 37 (1959), 215–220

SCOTT-TAGGART, M. J. "Butler on Disinterested Actions,"
Phil. Quart., 18 (1968), 16–28

SELLARS, R. W. "Guided Causality, Using Reason, and 'Free
Will,' " *J. Phil.*, 54 (1957), 485–493

–"The Levels of Causality: The Emergence of Guidance and
Reason in Nature," *Phil. Phenomenol. Res.*, 20 (1959–60),
1–17

SELLARS, WILFRID. "Mind, Meaning, and Behavior,"
Philosophical Studies, 3 (1952), 83–95

– *Science, Perception and Reality*. London: Routledge & Kegan
Paul, 1963

–"Imperatives, Intentions, and the Logic of 'Ought,' " in
Castañeda and Nakhnikian, 1965, pp. 159–218

– (a) "Fatalism and Determinism," in Lehrer, 1966, pp.
141–174

– (b) "Thought and Action," in Lehrer, 1966, pp. 105–139

SHARVEY, RICHARD. "A Logical Error in Taylor's 'Fatalism,' "
Analysis, 23 (1962–63), 96

–"Tautology and Fatalism," *J. Phil.*, 61 (1964), 293–295

SHUFORD, HAYWARD R., JR. "Logical Behaviorism and
Intentionality," *Theoria*, 32 (1966), 246–251

SHUTE, CLARENCE. "The Dilemma of Determinism after
Seventy-Five Years," *Mind*, 70 (1961), 331–350

SHWAYDER, DAVID. *The Stratification of Behavior*. London:
Routledge & Kegan Paul, 1965

SIDORSKY, DAVID. "A Note on Three Criticisms of von
Wright," *J. Phil.*, 62 (1965), 739–742

SIEGEL, SIDNEY. See Davidson, Suppes, and Siegel, 1957

SIEGLER, FREDERICK A. "Unconscious Intentions," *Inquiry*, 10
(1967), 251–267

SILBER, JOHN R. "Human Action and the Language of
Volitions," *Proc. Arist. Soc.*, 64 (1963–64), 199–220

SIMON, HERBERT. "The Logic of Rational Decision," *Brit. J.
Phil. Sci.*, 16 (1965), 169–186

–"The Logic of Heuristic Decision Making" [with comments
by R. Binkley and N. Belnap, and rejoinder], in
Rescher, 1967, pp. 1–35

SKINNER, B. F. *Science and Human Behavior*. New York:
Macmillan, 1953

SKINNER, R. C. "Freedom of Choice," *Mind*, 72 (1963), 463-480

SLUGA, HANS. See Lucas and Sluga, 1967

SMART, J. J. C. "Reason and Conduct," *Philosophy*, 25 (1950), 209–224

–"Sensations and Brain Processes," *Phil. Rev.*, 68 (1959), 141–156

– (a) "Free-Will, Praise and Blame," *Mind*, 70 (1961), 291–306

– (b) *An Outline of a System of Utilitarian Ethics.* Melbourne: Melbourne University Press, 1961

– See Hamlyn and Smart, 1964

SMITH, C. I. "A Note on Choice and Virtue," *Analysis*, 17 (1956–57), 21–23

SMITH, F. V. "Instinct in the Explanation of Behaviour," *Austl. J. Phil.*, 23 (1945), 35–56

SOBEL, J. H. "Dummett on Fatalism," *Phil. Rev.*, 75 (1966), 78–90

SOSA, ERNEST. "Actions and Their Results," *Logique et Analyse*, 30 (1965), 111–125

–"On Practical Inference and the Logic of Imperatives," *Theoria*, 32 (1966), 211–223

SPARSHOTT, F. E. "The Concept of Purpose," *Ethics*, 72 (1961–62), 157–170

SPROTT, W. J. H. See Gallie, Sprott, and Mace, 1947

STALLKNECHT, NEWTON P., F. C. WADE, and W. EARLE. "Freedom and Existence: a Symposium," *Rev. Metaph.*, 9 (1955–56), 27–56

STENNER, ALFRED J. "On Predicting Our Future," *J. Phil.*, 61 (1964), 415–428

STERN, K. "Mr. Hampshire and Professor Hart on Intention: A Note," *Mind*, 68 (1959), 98–99

STOUTLAND, FREDERICK. "Basic Actions and Causality," *J. Phil.*, 65 (1968), 467–475

STRAWSON, P. F. *Individuals*. London: Methuen, 1959

STROLL, AVRUM, ed. *Epistemology*. New York: Harper and Row, 1967

SUPPES, PATRICK. See Davidson, Suppes, and Siegel, 1957

SUTHERLAND, N. S. "Motives as Explanations," *Mind*, 68 (1959), 145–159

SWAIN, M. See Lehrer, Roelofs, and Swain, 1967

SWIGGART, PETER. "Doing and Deciding to Do," *Analysis*, 23 (1962–63), 17–19

TAYLOR, CHARLES. *The Explanation of Behaviour.* London: Routledge & Kegan Paul, 1964

TAYLOR, PAUL W. " 'Need' Statements," *Analysis*, 19 (1958–59), 106–111

TAYLOR, RICHARD. " 'I Can,' " *Phil. Rev.*, 69 (1960), 78–89

–"Fatalism," *Phil. Rev.*, 71 (1962), 56–66

– (a) "Causation," *Monist*, 47 (1962–63), 287–313

– (b) "Fatalism and Ability," *Analysis*, 23 (1962–63), 25–27

–"A Note on Fatalism," *Phil. Rev.*, 72 (1963), 497–499

– (a) "Comment," *J. Phil.*, 61 (1964), 305–307 [on Cahn, 1964 and Sharvey, 1964]

– (b) Deliberation and Foreknowledge," *Amer. Phil. Quart.*, 1 (1964), 73–80

– (c) "Not Trying to Do the Impossible," *Austl. J. Phil.*, 42 (1964), 98–100

– (a) *Action and Purpose.* Englewood Cliffs, NJ: Prentice-Hall, 1966

– (b) "Prevention, Postvention and the Will," in Lehrer, 1966, 65–85

TEICHMANN, J. "Mental Cause and Effect," *Mind*, 70 (1961), 36–52

TEN, C. L. "Mill on Self-Regarding Actions," *Philosophy*, 43 (1968), 29–37

THALBERG, IRVING. "Abilities and Ifs," *Analysis*, 22 (1961–62), 121–126

–"Foreknowledge and Decisions in Advance," *Analysis*, 24 (1963–64), 49–54

– (a) "Emotion and Thought," *Amer. Phil. Quart.*, 1 (1964), 45–55

– (b) "Freedom of Action and Freedom of Will," *J. Phil.*, 61 (1964), 405–415

– (a) "Do We Cause Our Own Actions?" *Analysis*, 27 (1967), 196–201

– (b) See McCormick and Thalberg, 1967

THOMAS, GEORGE B. "He Could Not Have Chosen Otherwise,"
S. J. Phil., 5 (1967), 269–274
TOLMAN, E. J. *Purposive Behavior in Animals and Men.*
Berkeley and Los Angeles: University of California Press,
1949
– *Behavior and Psychological Man.* Berkeley and Los Angeles:
University of California Press, 1961
TOULMIN, S. "The Logical Status of Psycho-Analysis,"
Analysis, 9 (1948–49), 23–29
TURQUET, P. M. See Farrell, Turquet, and Wisdom, 1962

URMSON, J. O. See Peters, McCracken, and Urmson, 1952

VESEY, G. N. A. "Volition," *Philosophy*, 36 (1961), 352–365
–"Agent and Spectator: The Double Aspect Theory," in
Royal Institute of Philosophy, 1968, pp. 139–159
VON WRIGHT, GEORG H. (a) *Norm and Action: A Logical
Enquiry.* New York: Humanities Press, 1963
– (b) "Practical Inference," *Phil. Rev.*, 72 (1963), 159–179
–"The Logic of Action – a Sketch" [with comments by
R. M. Chisholm and J. Robison, and rejoinder], in Rescher,
1967, pp. 121–146
– *An Essay in Deontic Logic and the General Theory of Action.*
[*Acta Philosophica Fennica, Fasc. XXI.*] Amsterdam: North
Holland, 1968

WADE, F. C. See Stallknecht, Wade, and Earle, 1955–56
WALLACE, JAMES D. "Pleasure as an End of Action," *Amer. Phil.
Quart.*, 3 (1966), 312–316
WALSH, J. See Morgenbesser and Walsh, 1962
–"Remarks on *Thought and Action*," *J. Phil.*, 60 (1963), 57–65
WALSH, W. H. "Historical Causation," *Proc. Arist. Soc.*, 63
(1962–63), 217–236
WALTON, K. A. "Rational Action," *Mind*, 76 (1967), 537–547
WAND, BERNARD. "Intelligibility and Free Choice," *Dialogue*, 1
(1962–63), 239–258
–"Uncertainty and Free Choice: a Reply," *Dialogue*, 3
(1964–65), 171–175

WARNOCK, MARY and A. C. EWING. "Symposium: The Justification of Emotions," *Proc. Arist. Soc. Supp.*, 31 (1957), 43–74

WEITZ, MORRIS. "Professor Ryle's 'Logical Behaviorism,' " *J. Phil.*, 48 (1951), 297–301

WHEATLEY, J. M. O. "Wishing and Hoping," *Analysis*, 18 (1957–58), 121–131

–"Hampshire on Human Freedom," *Phil. Quart.*, 12 (1962), 248–260

WHITE, A. R. "The Language of Motives," *Mind*, 67 (1958), 258–263

–"Inclination," *Analysis*, 21 (1960–61), 40–42

– *Explaining Human Behaviour*. Hull: Hull University Publications, 1962

– *The Philosophy of Mind*. New York: Random House, 1967

– (a) "On Being Obliged to Act," in Royal Institute of Philosophy, 1968, pp. 64–82

– (b) *The Philosophy of Action*. Oxford: Oxford University Press, 1968

WHITE, MORTON. *Foundations of Historical Knowledge*. New York: Harper and Row, 1965

WHITELEY, C. H. "Behaviorism," *Mind*, 70 (1961), 164–174

–" 'Can,' " *Analysis*, 23 (1962–63), 91–93

– See Haksar and Whiteley, 1966

–"Mental Causes," in Royal Institute of Philosophy, 1968, pp. 98–114

WHITTIER, D. B. "Causality and the Self," *Monist*, 49 (1965), 290–303

WILD, JOHN. *Existence and the World of Freedom*. Englewood Cliffs, NJ: Prentice-Hall, 1963

–"Reply to Professor Frankena," *Phil. Phenomenol. Res.*, 27 (1966–67), 97–102

WILKINS, B. T. "The Thing to Do," *Mind*, 74 (1965), 89–91

WILL, F. L. "Intention, Error and Responsibility," *J. Phil.*, 61 (1964), 171–179

WILLIAMS, C. J. F. (a) "Comment on Professor MacKay's Reply," *Analysis*, 21 (1960–61), 84–85

– (b) "Logical Indeterminacy and Freewill," *Analysis*, 21 (1960–61), 12–13

WILLIAMS, D. C. "Remarks on Causation and Compulsion,"
J. Phil., 50 (1953), 120–124

WILLIAMS, GARDNER. "Logical and Natural Compulsion in Free
Will," *J. Phil.*, 42 (1945), 185–191

–"Freedom of Choice in the Pre-Determined Future," *Phil.
Phenomenol. Res.*, 12 (1951–52), 130–134

–"The Natural Causation of Human Freedom," *Phil.
Phenomenol. Res.*, 19 (1958–59), 529–531

WILSON, H. V. R. "Causal Discontinuity in Fatalism and
Indeterminism," *J. Phil.*, 52 (1955), 70–72

WILSON, JOHN. "Freedom and Compulsion," *Mind*, 67 (1958),
68–69

WINCH, PETER. *The Idea of a Social Science*. London:
Routledge & Kegan Paul, 1963

–"Wittgenstein's Treatment of the Will," *Ratio*, 10 (1968),
38–53

WISDOM, J. O. See Farrell, Turquet, and Wisdom, 1962

WISDOM, W. A. "On How Donnellan Knows What He Is
Doing," *J. Phil.*, 60 (1963), 589–590

WITTGENSTEIN, LUDWIG. *Philosophical Investigations*, translated
by G. E. M. Anscombe. Oxford: Blackwell, 1953

YOLTON, JOHN W. "Ascriptions, Descriptions and Action
Sentences," *Ethics*, 67 (1956–57), 307–310

–"Act and Circumstance," *J. Phil.*, 59 (1962), 337–350

–"Agent Causality," *Amer. Phil. Quart.*, 3 (1966), 14–26

Index

This book

was designed by

ANTJE LINGNER

under the direction of

ALLAN FLEMING

Lightning Source UK Ltd.
Milton Keynes UK
UKHW010015210722
406167UK00002B/430